A SINGLE WOMAN'S FOCUS

Every Ruth Needs a Naomi

Carla R. Cannon

A SINGLE WOMAN'S FOCUS

Every Ruth Needs a Naomi

Carla R. Cannon

Printed in the United States of America

Book Cover Designed By: Bobby Barnhill

Editing Services Provided By: W.E. Da Cruz/Rain Publishing

First Printing, 2014

ISBN-13: 9781500261771
ISBN-10: 1500261777

Ordering Information:

Quantity Sales; Special discounts are available on quantity purchases by corporations, associations, and others. For details, contact Carla R. Cannon at Carla@WomenOfStandard.org or call 919-525-0665.

Dedication:

I dedicate this book to Rhonda Harper. Know that you are special and God has a unique plan for your life. You are not a mistake and you were created to be victorious. Be encouraged and know that God promises to fill every void in your life and the moment you stop seeking it through things and others, He will grant your very heart's desire. Know that I love you and you will forever be in my prayers. I believe in you.

Table of Contents:

A Letter to My Sisters

To every single woman who has ever felt as if you were you unworthy to be loved, or as if you were damaged goods I want you to know that you deserve to be loved and that God has someone He created just for you. I want to encourage you not to give up but to take your mind off of finding a man and focus your attention on finding "you."

It is when you as a single woman begin to change your focus from what you desire to what God desires and allow Him to fill every void that lies within that you will find true contentment. During the process of being content where you are, God is molding and shaping you into the wife you were created to be. He is also preparing not a perfect mate, but the best mate for you who will compliment your purpose and assignment while here on earth.

During your singleness I invite you to take this time and begin to work on you. Allow God to show you areas which require improvement or areas i which you can enhance or make better. Maybe it involves making an attitude adjustment, developing better spending habits, reaching your ide weight, learning a new craft, launching a new business; whatever it is do for you and allow the joy of the Lord to fill your soul while doing. You never want your reason for getting married to be because you *need* a mar but because you have reached a level in life which requires his assistanc to catapult you into the next dimension in God and the same for him as i relates to you. Within the pages of this book it is my prayer that you will leave behind all carnal thoughts and behaviors and get in tune with the Holy Spirit.

When you quiet your spirit, the Lord will speak to you. He will answer questions you have always longed to know. He will comfort you in area you may feel alone. He will fill you with joy, contentment and ease when other single women are anxious and in a hurry to find their *Mr. Right*.

Instead of trying to find him, you will be positioning yourself to be found. Therefore, during this time embrace your process and learn how to properly love yourself. It is impossible to give what you don't possess. It's also challenging to accept love when you are not accustomed to receiving it.

This is why I encourage you to develop a solid relationship with our Heavenly Father, Jesus because in return He will fill every void, cleanse you from the inside out and transform you into the wife you were created to be for your husband. We see this manifested in the biblical story of Ruth when she meets and marries Boaz.

Know that I wrote this book with you in mind. All of your questions, silent struggles and tears I understand for I am certain you will find yourself within the pages of this book. This journey is one you do not have to travel alone for we have the Lord indeed, but we also have each other.

Love,

Carla

Foreword

By: Pastor John Lofton

If you are looking for a feel-good book that is complicit in perpetuating dysfunctional sinful behavior, then *A Single Woman's Focus* may not be the book for you. If you are interested in reading a book where the content is non-threatening, non-challenging and unchanging, this is not the book for you. If you are looking to read a book that will endorse nominal and mediocre Christian living, this is not the book for you. If you are looking to read a book filled with half-truths about Christian integrity and godliness and whole lies about real relationships defined by culture, this is not the book for you.

However, if you are ready to read a book that will show you key ways to overcome a defeatism mentality and challenge you to live a godly purpose driven life, then this is the book for you. If you are looking for real life examples and tools to keep you in a perpetual state of joy and peace, this is the book for you. If you are looking for a book that will empower you to face your fears and take hold of a courageous resolve to see how fearfully and wonderfully you have been created, then this is definitely the book for you.

Carla Cannon has a way of taking her life's unexpected experiences and transform them into practical and relevant nuggets for living. She truly lives what she writes and is able to transfer her passion from her heart through the pen to the page. She encourages women to protect the most valuable gift they possess.....themselves.

You will learn that one is a whole number and you do not need a man to complete you, you are already complete in Christ. She challenges single women to confront feelings of fear, loneliness, unimportance, helplessness, complacency and sadness so they can reach their full potential in God. She will free you from believing the lies of the enemy that you have to settle for his worse (Bozo) when God is preparing you for His best (Boaz). This is a well-rounded read providing viewpoints from single men and from couples for a marital perspective.

As your read through the pages of this mind-transforming, heart-changing work, allow the Holy Spirit to speak to your spirit about those areas that need to be re-aligned, re-shaped or relinquished. You will sense Carla's heart to see every single woman triumph over every setback in their lives and reach the ultimate prize only found in Jesus Christ. Once you find Him, He will lead the right man to you. Carla is not only a powerful and anointed business woman, empowerment coach, author and minister of the Gospel, she is also a great mother and my spiritual daughter.

Single ladies, it is time to get focused. So, sit back in your comfortable chair, get a hot cup of coffee or tea and allow the peace (Shalom) of God to fill your heart, mind and spirit where you will have nothing missing, nothing lacking and nothing broken in your lives!

Pastor John F. Lofton
Senior Pastor - Covenant Community Church   www.ChangeAtC3.org

Preface:

The Story of Ruth
The Importance of Positioning

Ruth 1-4

In the days when the judges ruled, there was a famine in the land and a certain man of Bethlehem of Judah named, Elimelech went to sojourn in the country of Moab along with his wife, Naomi and two sons, Mahlon and Chilion. Later Elimelech died and Naomi was left with their two sons who eventually married two women named Orpah and Ruth. They remained there for ten years after the passing of Naomi's husband.

Later the two sons died as well and Naomi summoned the ladies to return back to their mother's house and both of her daughter-in-laws, Orpah and Ruth cried. Orpah eventually left and returned back to her mother, however, Ruth clung to her.

Naomi tried to convince Ruth to return back to her homeland as well but Ruth continued to refuse and told Naomi that wherever she went, she would go as well and that her people would become her people also and that her God would also be her God.

Overall Ruth had grown attached to Naomi and refused to detach herself from her. She chose to remain and suffer with Naomi in this process of grieving over her loss sons rather than returning to her homeland which would have provided comfort and stability however, Ruth's loyalty to Naomi outweighed her current discomfort.

Naomi had a kinsman of her husband's who was a man of wealth and of the family of Elimelech, whose name was, Boaz. Ruth, proved to be a hard worker, began to glean in a field after the reapers, and she happene to stop at the part of a field belonging to Boaz. He then noticed Ruth and inquired about her.

Notice here that Ruth was not out trying to be seen nor was she worrying about being found, but she was simply focused on surviving and doing right by her mother-in-law. Ruth was a woman on a mission who in return was sought after by a man whom we would deem as *Mr. Right*.

While inquiring about Ruth, Boaz learned about her loyalty to Naomi and instead of having her work in the field uncovered, he ordered his men to watch her and leave handfuls of grain behind for her on purpose as she worked. After learning whose field Ruth had been working in Naomi advised her to wash and anoint herself, put on her finest apparel, and lay at his feet once he laid down for the evening.

Boaz, being startled out of his sleep saw Ruth lying at his feet and he blessed her stating that she did not go after young men whether rich or poor. He began to praise her for the great works she had done in which he had been informed of in regards to her love toward Naomi.

To sum up the story which was only four chapters long, Ruth was strategically placed in the field belonging to Boaz by God who had a great plan for her life. The two of them later birthed a son, Obed who was the father of Jesse, who was the father of David, who later became a king and was in the lineage of Jesus.

Therefore, Boaz and Ruth became part of Jesus' lineage and the great-grandparents of a king which would not have taken place if Ruth had not followed the instructions (or heeded to the wisdom) of Naomi.

We should never believe in coincidences but be reminded that our steps are ordered by the Lord and He has a great plan for each of our lives. This is why I recommend that you surround yourself with seasoned women who are older than you are, have more experiences than you and who have overcome some things in their life. When you do this you will gain insight on the path you are currently traveling for there's nothing like having your own personal tour guide through life. Sure your Naomi (woman of wisdom) may not be able to guide you the full course of the way but she can provide a blueprint that is in alignment with God's word that if followed will bless your life greatly.

I shared the story of Ruth to inform you as a single woman that it is vital to have a Naomi in your life. All of your friends can't be young, single and ignorant saying foolish things such as, *"Girl I don't need a man because I am I-N-D-E-P-E-N-D-E-N-T!"* That is foolishness and I advise you to stay away from those type of women and keep them out of your circle. Now, there is nothing wrong with being an independent woman but when you are so independent to the point that you fail to allow a man to be a man and you take on both roles then *"Houston we have a problem!"*

A wise woman knows she must keep a few seasoned women around her i she truly desires to be successful in life. The seasoned women are those whom I call "Naomi". That is why this book is called, *A Single Woman's Focus: Every Ruth Needs a Naomi.*

I am speaking to you my sister as if you are Ruth and encouraging you to get connected to not just one Naomi but I pray the Lord sends you a few wise women who will assist you in your process of preparation and positioning as Naomi did for Ruth as she led her to Boaz.

I do not want to discourage you from having other single friends but if you are going to have single friends you want to ensure they too are women of wisdom, who are positioning as well as preparing themselves for their husbands and have vowed to do things God's way. Even if they are single women who are content in their singleness and do not desire husbands, you want to ensure your circle is filled with women who hono and take heed to the Word of God in their lives.

A Single Woman's Focus: Every Ruth Needs a Naomi is to help bring single women back to a place where God is their first love and they learr how to submit to and fall in love with Him. I am a firm believer that if w can remain committed to Christ, then we will indeed be faithful to our husband when he shows up.

It is my prayer that you would listen attentively as I share wisdom I've learned as a single woman who has been through various processes as it relates to dating, being single, wrestling in my identity, being single again and now dating again.

What a process right? My story doesn't end in wedding bells (not yet anyway) but prayerfully part II of this book will have a Cinderella ending but for now I am a single sister just like you sharing how I maintain focus and commit to doing things God's way, while allowing Him to develop me into the woman I was created to be.

There are so many things that require our focus therefore we can't afford to sit around watching the clock asking questions such as, *"When Lord when?"* or making the mistake of questioning whether every man who holds a door for you, compliments you or even says hello to you with a smile is your husband.

A Single Woman's Focus is here to set you free and cleanse you from anxiousness, impatience, discontentment, anxiety and even desperation. Sadly many women are desperate for love and will settle for anything to receive even the slightest bit of attention from a man even if it means compromising in the process. The man God has for you is worth waiting for and in the end you will be glad you waited.

Introduction

A Single Woman's Focus: Every Ruth Needs a Naomi is a book that was birthed out of several painful relationships I have endured which left me empty, frustrated and full of tears and anxiety wondering if God was ever going to send a man who would genuinely love me for me.

I like many women often searched for love in all of the wrong place. Wha I didn't know was that I was actually searching for my father while thinking I was in dying need of a husband. Yes, I know that's deep therefore please allow me to explain.

See, I never knew why every man I dated was always ten plus years olde than me. I thought I liked the maturity and stability that came from men o this caliber for the guys my age seemed to have only one thing in mind......SEX.

Surprisingly many of the older men were the exact same way. They appeared to be nice and to have it going on whether financially, appearance wise and to top it off I really thought one guy was the one when he stayed all night and did not get up to leave in the middle of the night while I was sleeping.

Now, don't act like you don't know what I'm talking about. I told you my first book, *The Power in Waiting* was only a sneak peek into my life but am keeping it all the way real in this book. I am going to hit every topic the Lord brings to my mind in an effort to help you become free as a single woman knowing there is nothing lacking, broken or missing from your life.

Too often we allow others to dictate our happiness and because we are attractive, successful and handling our business people look at us as to say, *"Where yo' man at?"* Funny thing is we were finally content and at peace until that last comment from one of the mothers at our church or a family member whom we hadn't seen in a while asks, *"You ain't marrie yet!"*

I'm here to tell you that just because you are single does not mean you are incomplete. I'm kind of getting ahead of myself but I felt the need to say this early on because too often we feel if our life doesn't measure up to our neighbors, or sister girl down the street who *appears* to have it all then we make the mistake of comparing ourselves which is the worst thing we could ever do.

The reason why this is so dangerous is because you don't have a clue what sister girl is dealing with to keep her man, her house, her car or perhaps even her dog! Everything that glitters *ain't* gold and you must stop comparing yourself to other women.

Rule # 1: Do not compare yourself to another woman. You are enough and you are beautiful with all you have to offer and your Man of God will find you in due time (God's appointed time).

The purpose of this book is to not only encourage you as a single woman but to share wisdom as it relates to different topics such as: *"What do I do while I wait for my husband?" "What is the appropriate way to date?" "Should I date someone from my church?" "What's really wrong with masturbation if I am not having sex with a physical person?" "How do I overcome loneliness?"*

Within this book I am going to answer all of those questions and more! My goal is to uplift you out of the place of anxiousness, wondering when your time will come and bring peace to your mind knowing that just because you are single that does not mean there is something wrong with you!

Rule #2: Just because you are single that does not mean there is something wrong with you! Declare aloud: *"There is nothing lacking, broken or missing in my life!"*

Be assured that you have picked up the right book and although I do not have all of the answers I have experienced enough to share with you what works and what you should avoid. Now, I can't force you to listen to me for I am only here to serve as a mentor in your life to help you avoid some of the heartache I had to face and bring encouragement to you to remind you that it is going to happen!

Rule #3: No matter how you feel, never doubt! Always speak life and be led by the Holy Spirit and not your emotions. Declare aloud: *"It is going to happen!"* If you desire to be married trust me, you don't have to try to make it happen, it will happen in God's timing.

How to Get the Most out of This Book: Approach this book with an open mind because I may challenge the ways you have been taught or believed to be true. Get ready for some serious down to earth girl talk. I intentionally wrote this book as if you and I were sitting on a sofa sharing hot tea (my favorite) from Star bucks having a serious heart to heart.

This book will serve as a guide and source of empowerment whenever you are tempted to give up and jump into the sheets with a man who is no your husband. We must get away from compromising to avoid the holida blues or to make ourselves *feel good.* I'd much rather be alone than to have a man lay up with me knowing I am not the only woman he is making love to. How many women are compromising and sharing a man because they have embraced the concept, *"a man is better than no man a all?"* I'm sure there are hundreds of women doing this but it doesn't have to be you.

You are worth so much more therefore to get the most out of this book you must say the declarations out loud, journal your thoughts and share this book with another single friend who may be battling loneliness or perhaps has an issue in which she may feel no one understands. Allow h to read this book with you and the two of you enjoy it and become heale together.

How to Know If This Book Is for You: If you are a woman who is content in your singleness and do not desire a husband nor do you strug in your flesh, then my sister perhaps you should be writing this book an should be reading it!

The women this book is for are those who are tired of putting on the church face, shouting all over the place and know they are still going home to Fred, Bobby, Steven or Tim who are not their husbands. They are acting as a wife by having the man up in their sheets and you really want him out but perhaps you have never been without a man.

Or maybe you are a woman where fornication with a man is not your issue at all. Maybe you desire the same sex and can't seem to find your way out of that situation because you really do want to become free. If this is you I want to direct you back to my first book, *The Power in Waiting* where I share my story of overcoming homosexuality and how my deliverance was a process and did not take place instantaneously. *The Power in Waiting* deals a lot with the process and how to embrace it in order to transform into who God has created you to be. If this is you, then this book is not for you just yet, read *The Power in Waiting*, then come back to this book.

If you are single and seeking contentment, have unanswered questions and desire a husband then you have picked up the right book! Get ready lady because this is about to be one ride that will set your mind free, calm your spirit and release unconditional joy in your life! In the words of a special woman: *"Know that you is smart, you is kind and you is important!"* Now let's go!

Chapter One
Mistakes Single Women Make

It is my hope that you understand my purpose in sharing the story of Ruth but just in case you have yet to grasp it let me further explain. When the Lord laid it upon my heart to write a book for single women to empower, encourage as well as educate them I received what I like to call a spiritual download and the title, *A Single Woman's Focus* immediately came to my mind.

Now of course it was natural for the story of Ruth to make sense for many know how she was favored by Boaz who found her focused on making a living for herself along with her mother-in-law, Naomi.

Another story that comes to mind along with Ruth is the story of Esther (Found in the book of Esther in the Holy Bible) which to me Ruth displays the importance of positioning and Esther displays the importance of preparation.

Positioning and preparation are vitally important if you are to transition from being a single woman to becoming a wife. Webster's Dictionary defines the word *positioning* as: *"to put or arrange (someone or something) in a particular place or way."* It goes on to define the word *preparation* as: *"the action or process of making ready or being ready for use or consideration."*

Mistake # 1: One mistake many single women make is they fail to prepare and position themselves for the husbands they desire.

Let's begin with positioning. which again is defined as *"to put or arrange someone or something in a particular place or way."* To be positioned means to simply be strategically placed in a way that you can be found by your husband. We are made aware in Proverbs 18:22, that a man who finds a wife finds a good thing and obtains favor from the Lord. Now there are two things that stand out to me in that text: and that is, *"a man that finds a wife"* and *"finds a good thing."*

My concern with some women today is instead of getting in position to be found many tend to be so busy trying to gain the attention of men whether through exotic clothing (which society calls sexy) or attention seeking habits such as being loud to be seen or heard. Later in this book you are going to hear from two single men of different backgrounds and professions (one guy operates in ministry and another is a successful business man) who share what really turn men off about women and I urge you to take heed to the wisdom they are sharing.

As single women one thing I want you to understand is men are hunters by nature and whatsoever they desire, they will go after.

Point # 1: Never chase a man for men are hunters by nature therefore if he is truly interested he does not need your assistance in approaching you.

So often I hear women say things such as, *"Girl he was shy so I just asked for his number."* No, the truth is if he really wanted your number, trust and believe he would ask you for it.

I can recall watching the movie, Stomp the Yard and DJ (played by Columbus Short) admired April (played by Meagan Good) and all it took was for him to see her one time and immediately he felt he had to have her.

There was a scene in the movie where he was in line waiting to purchase his books for college and you know how long those lines can be during registration. But she walked by, captured his attention therefore, he got out of line trying to find her and although he couldn't at the time due to the crowd; the point is he was willing to sacrifice his place in line to find her.

He later ran into her again and found out she had a boyfriend who was mistreating her. To grasp her attention he (being the newbie or freshman in college) took it upon himself to battle her boyfriend during a dance off and took everyone by surprise even her with how gifted he was.

If you think that was impressive guess what else he did. Because she would not give him the time of day during a quick conversation one day he asked her to dinner and her response was pretty much that she had a boyfriend. However, knowing she was being mistreated by this guy he began to ask her again and she replied, *"I can't. I'm tutoring."* April really was trying to do the right thing by remaining faithful to her boyfriend. When DJ asked what she was tutoring she walked off.

Now, do you think that stopped DJ? Absolutely not! Remember I told you men are hunters by nature therefore they do not need our help in the process of pursuing us. If he wants you bad enough he will come over and talk to you. If he wants you bad enough he will inquire about who you are; real men are never scared however, some may be quite patient. While you think he is not paying you any attention he may have actually been watching you on the job or at church; etc.

Back to Stomp the Yard:

So after having a second encounter with this beautiful woman, DJ took it upon himself to locate the building where he could sign up for tutoring. When asked what subject he desired to be tutored in his response was, "What subject does April Palmer tutor?" The lady replied, *"History."* His response to her was, *"History it is."*

As April arrived at the library to prepare for a tutoring session with a student, completely unaware of the trouble this guy went through to find her, better yet or that he was the one she was to be tutoring for this session! In walks DJ and she is totally surprised by his many efforts to capture her attention.

Long story short, guess how he ends up getting her to go out on a date with him? During one of their tutoring sessions DJ challenges April by asking her to ask him anything from the history lesson and if he got it right she would have to go out with him to dinner that night. Being certain that he would not know the answer to what she thought was a very challenging question, she took him up on his offer.

April goes on and asks him a very challenging question, and DJ begins to flip through the history book as if he was searching for the answer. April then said, *"Maybe some other time."* Out of the blue, DJ answered her question very intelligently and the movie captured total amazement in which she displayed all over her face with a huge smile because this guy whom she thought was some *"hood boy"* (because of his appearance) was more educated than he appeared to be. I'm sure you know how the story ends. You got it! DJ and April went to dinner and the rest is history. He ended up stealing her away from her boyfriend.

Mistake # 2: Don't judge a man by his exterior. A "God's man" is not chosen by your flesh but by your spirit.

So often, we as women make the mistake of focusing more so on temporal things such as how big his shoe size is, what kind of car he driving, what type of swagger he has, how tall he is and so forth. Truthfully our attention should be more on things which uphold value and that truly matter such as how is his walk with the Lord, what are his dreams, goals and aspirations, how does he treat his mother. These are questions of value that we need to consider that we often overlook and neglect due to being attracted to the exterior of a man.

Being focused on the outer appearance of a man will mess you up! I remember one guy I dated, he was just what I liked: tall, muscular, big feet (ha!), slightly bowlegged and had a killer smile to go with the entire package. I told you there is no patty caking in this book. In order to get free we have to keep it all the way real and tell the truth! I told you that you weren't alone.

He and I began as really good friends and our friendship developed throughout the years then all of a sudden one year out the blue we decided to date. Now mind you because of my immature mind all I could focus on was how we looked together as a couple, how good the sex was and how I felt others would receive us as a couple.

If I may be very candid here, this man could sex me like I had never been sexed before, placed me in positions I had never been in, made my body respond in ways it had never responded before but guess what? It was all a set up!

After being involved with this man sexually that was one of the hardest soul ties I ever had to break in my life. There was rarely a time I saw this man that we did not have sex. I could so relate to Nina (played by Nia Long) in the movie, *Love Jones* when she was sharing her sexual experience with her girlfriend about Darius (played by Larenz Tate). She told her friend, *"It was as if it talked to me."* Her friend then asked her, *"What did it say?"* Nina then tells her it said, *"Niiiiiiiiiiiiiiiiiiiiinnnnnnnnnnnnnnnaaaaaaa!"*

When I first saw this movie I thought that part was hilarious and if you have seen the movie then you know exactly what I am talking about. Making love to this man was as if every part of my body (even my toes) responded to his touch. But again it was a set up because each time I would be intimate with him the deeper the soul tie would develop and the harder it was to break away from him. I would change my number then end up giving it to him. I'm sure you are laughing here because you may have been guilty of that too. Good sex will make you do some crazy things. Whoo! But we thank the Lord for deliverance! Amen to that!

I tell women all the time to be careful what you ask for because the same way the Lord is listening so is the enemy. Satan studies us, and he learns what we like and don't like and he creates packages that will attract us to get us off course and keep us from our destiny.

Point # 2: *Rid yourself of carnal prayers focused on the exterior of a mate; but focus on eternal qualities such as him being a man of prayer, integrity, character, a provider, a protector, a father to your children; et*

In the midst of all this good love making one thing I failed to mention to you and that is this guy was still *married.* Yep! He and his wife had been separated for years but the truth is they never finalized their divorce. So here I was not only committing adultery because legally and according to the Word of God this man was still bound to his wife!

Here's a topic we don't like to talk about often. We feel that if a man is separated from his wife then he is available to date us. Absolutely not! Until the divorce is final and he is no longer bound to her legally you need to leave that man where he is. Truth is, I desired a husband but marriage was the last thing on his mind. Guess why? Because he was already married! While he was dating me if he wanted to go back to his wife at any given time he could have because legally she was still his wife and there would have been nothing I could do about it.

I thank the Lord for not allowing me to become pregnant during the process of dealing with this man but I also do not regret the experience. It helped me become a better woman and that is why I am able to write this book to you to encourage you not to get caught up on how cute others say the two of you look together, or how handsome he may be. You want a man of moral character, integrity and one who is as in love with God as you are!

Point # 3: Date someone because you like them, not because others like him.

The opinions of others really don't matter because the covenant you will make with your spouse will be between you, him and God and you are vowed to honor that covenant relationship until death do you part.

I was more focused on what others would think of us as a couple because in my mind, he was so fine, not to mention also a great father to his children. But even up to this day I believe the Lord allowed me to settle for that man for a short season to allow me to identify broken areas within myself that needed healing. This man was double my age and did not have it together but I was tempted to settle because we had been friends for so long therefore he knew me rather intimately. Sadly though when I think back, although we had been friends for years I didn't know too many intimate details about him but I was so quick to share my inner secrets with him. That was another mistake I made.

Another painful mistake I made was not having the adequate amount of self-love to know that I deserved to be the only lady, not the number three lady. I failed to mention that not only was he married but he was also seeing another woman when he and I decided to *"date"* in which he was supposed to cut things off with the other woman which even until this day I am not sure if he really did or not.

Mistake #3: Women get caught up in having "good sex" with a man in which later taints your vision, opens you up to his spirit and now your vision is blurred and you can no longer see clearly because you opened Pandora's Box and drank from the cup.

Ladies, we must know that we are worth being pursued and sought after. Remember men do not need our help. Even the shyest man will go and get coached before he allows the woman he is truly interested in to get away from him.

Point # 3: While dating a man keep your legs closed because opening them not opens up your natural body to him but also your spirit.

Sex is more spiritual than it is natural for even after the man is gone his spirit will still remain. You will be left to deal with your own issues as well as all the stuff he dumped into your spirit. Keep your spirit clean ladies, it's not worth it!

Mistake # 4: Another common mistake I see many women make is being more focused on the list instead of applying that same energy on actually becoming the list.

So often we have things written down such as, he must drive this type of car, make this amount of money, his credit score must be above a specific number, he has to be toned and in shape, no kids; and so on.

Meanwhile our money doesn't match what we have written down for him, our credit score is so terrible that some of us put cell phones and light bills in our child's name which is very pathetic if I may add. Our tummy isn't flat and our arms aren't toned, and we have more than one child and so forth.

Point # 4: *Focus on becoming the list you so often create for your desired spouse.*

My point is instead of creating this long list for your spouse to measure up to, why not focus on becoming the list because the truth is you are what you attract. I attracted broken men because I was broken. I attracted men who were full of lust because I was full of lust.

Don't ever fool yourself in to thinking the issue only resides with the other person. If you are woman who attracts undercover homosexual men, it is now time to identify what it is on the inside of you that attracts those types of men.

If you constantly attract womanizers or abusive men locate where that is coming from within you in order to pull it up by the root to rid yourself of that spirit that causes others to be able to identify that you have low self-esteem or lack confidence.

Trust me men can spoke a weak woman a mile away just as many of us can spot a man who actually bats for the other team but we are so caught up on how he makes he feel sexually that we miss the tell-tale signs of him being accustomed to male lovers.

I told you this was not a play-play book if we are going to be real to get free from some stuff then I must expose all of it. That means sister it is safe for you to take off your mask. I am willing to expose myself to help you become free. I want you to know you are not alone. I have dated someone I knew had wrestled with homosexuality and he would cry often about really desiring to be totally free and because I had gone through that I thought I could deal with it and again because I was a broken and lonely woman and the last man I had dated told me no one would ever love me like he did, I actually believed that and almost settled for a man who was a preacher but yet still battling in his identity.

My God! I feel God's anointing here. See, the enemy don't want me to share this type of stuff because he is afraid you may get free and finally come out with your stuff in an effort to help others become free!

Point # 5: *Whatsoever is hidden in the dark possesses power over you, but whatsoever you shine light on and expose, you now have power over it!*

Never be ashamed of your story and never be afraid to admit that you are broken, lonely, wounded, angry or afraid. There is nothing wrong with feeling this way it is only unhealthy to remain that way. The good news is there is help and I am here to walk through this process with you.

You are not alone. There are other women who have made it out of what you are in and you can come out too! Whether you have made some of the mistakes I have mentioned above or not know that you are not identified by your issue for your issue doesn't define who you are!

Point # 6: *I am not what I am currently dealing with! My current situation does not dictate my destiny!*

Let's elaborate more about the importance of preparation and positioning. Remember I said, according to Webster's Dictionary, the word *preparation* is defined as *"the action or process of making ready or being ready for use or consideration."*

Mistake # 5: Another mistake many single women make is they will pray for a husband but they won't prepare for his arrival.

How often do we pray for things and while we are waiting for them to come to pass we fail to prepare for it? Wouldn't it be a tragedy that if everything we prayed to God for He immediately granted it to us?

In my previous book, *The Power in Waiting,* I talk about the promises of God and the manifestation but what lies in between the two is the inevitable process and that is the part in which many get lost, lose focus or sadly, even give up.

Point # 7: *Receiving a gift from God without proper preparation can end in tragedy. Commit to spending time preparing for what you desire God to do in your life.*

It is during your waiting that you become equipped and great characteristics such as: patience, self-control and character are developed within you. It is also during your waiting that you undergo great training of how to become an excellent wife. You don't want to just be a wife but you want to be the best wife and the "good thing" your husband will desire.

Sadly nowadays we have reality shows which have practically overtaken our television networks such as Basketball Wives and Love & Hip which have done such a poor job displaying marriages or even the process of dating God's way.

Within these various shows we see the love and greed of money where individuals get married for social status or put up with infidelity in order to enjoy the lavish lifestyle of the rich and famous. Sadly, many women settle for this outcome to prevent them from going back to their previous lifestyles of *not enough.* I'd rather live in a one bedroom apartment with rats and roaches than to live in luxury with a man humping up and down on me but then out doing God knows what with other women. It is truly time to uplift a standard and take our power back as women.

To become a wife and marry a great man of God, preparation is key because it is vital for us very important because I believe as women it is vital that we know our place. Our place is to stand by our men, allowing them to lead the way for the set man God has for you is to be the head of the home as well as the provider and the protector.

However, because many of us have become accustomed to raising our kids, cooking dinner, cleaning the house, reviewing homework, working on projects, getting the kids off to their soccer games, and taking out the trash, we often forget when a real man shows up we no longer have to carry all of the weight alone.

As women we must rid ourselves of the word, I-N-D-E-P-E-N-D-E-N-T. I believe that is the worst thing Rap Artist, Lil Boosie and R & B singer, Neyo could have ever done was create songs of this nature to encourage women to take on this attitude of being super independent.

Now don't get me wrong as a single woman you should be handling your business, taking care of your children if you have them, riding in the best and living in the best. But when your man of God shows up you also need to know how to take the submissive role and ensure he feels needed, important and treated as the King of your home.

Mistake #6: Women often make the mistake of saying, *"I don't need a man for nothing!"* Sadly there are a lot of women who have adapted this philosophy that the only thing a man is good for is what lies between his legs and what's in his wallet which is the furthest from the truth.

It is important that we understand men are vital to our lives and it is for more reasons than to sex us real good all day and night. The man God has for you will compliment the vision and purpose the Lord has for you.

Now don't get me wrong good sex is a part of the package however, it should not be the main focus of our desire to have a mate which prayerfully will develop into a marriage.

Point # 8: The mate God has for you should have much more to offer you than what he has between his legs.

I have never seen women than I do today who will settle for a brother w has no job, no car, neither does he have a pot to piss in nor a window to throw it out of (excuse my language) but he can come in and sex us real good and in the words of comedian, Sommore we in return will give him the key to all of our stuff.

He will have the key to our house where he pays absolutely no bills, we will even buy him a cell phone and have it put in our name, and don't even have access to his passcode to get into his phone. We will dress him and play the role of the man all in an effort to keep him.

Ladies don't get me wrong it's nothing wrong with doing things for your man especially if receiving gifts is his love language or yours. However, simply taking care of a man is completely out of question. Again, the man is to be the provider, the head and it is his duty to care for you and to ensure you have everything you need.

Now on the flip side of that, you must be willing to work with a man who is in his process. Now a dead beat man and a man in his process are two different people. Allow me to explain the difference: A dead beat man has yet to identify his purpose in life and is not even trying to. He does not have a job, lives with one of his home boys or better yet still at home with his mother with no dreams, goals or aspirations.

A man in his process is one who may not make a lot of money, drive the finest car, have the biggest house but he has "potential" . That's the key word that I want you to look for when you are dating and determining who is marriage material and who is not.

Mistake # 7: As single women we must understand that we too are in our process therefore we must not stick our noses up at a brother who is trying and actually has goals set in place to provide a better life for himself.

One thing about us as women, we were created to bring out the best in a man. We have that gift and the sooner we are able to identify the difference between a dead beat man and a man who has potential the sooner you will position yourself to be found by the man of your dreams.

Point # 9*: Know the difference between a dead beat man and a processed man.*

I recently had a conversation with an author of a very successful book and asked for his view as it related to some of the mistakes single women make. His response did not come as a shocker to me for it was something I noticed as well.

He mentioned the way many of us declare our independence so verbally which in turn, becomes a major turn off to men. He began to go on to say that of course a man desires a strong woman but not so strong to the point where the man is not needed or is led to feel as though he is in her shadow and has no true presence.

As I began to listen to this gentleman share his view on some mistakes women make, I was wowed by one of his comments because it was so true! Society teaches us to be strong and independent not needing anyone else to help us handle our business right? However, the Word of God teaches us that we were designed and created for relationships.

We must rid ourselves of songs with lyrics such as, *"All the women that's independent throw your hands up at me!"* Also, songs such as, *"Me, myself and I is all I got in the end, that's what I found out, and it ain't no need to cry, I took a vow that from now on I'm gonna be my own best friend!"* Don't believe there Christian women who are Bey (aka Beyonce fans you better think again! I know you knew that song!

How about songs with lyrics such as: *"I-N-D-E-P-E-N-D-E-N-T do you know what that mean? She got her own house, her own car…she a bad broad!"* It is songs like these that we as women take so literally which in return cause men (especially black men) to run away from black women Oops! Did I say that? Yes I did!

That's another thing I notice women of color as so quick to get an attitude when they see a African American man with a Caucasian woman, however, it is often times the behavior or the tendency to be needy which causes successful black men to look the other way.

Real men don't want to listen to you gossip all day on the phone. They do not want a dominating woman he controls the relationship. They also don't care for a woman who can handle it all on her own and has no need for him.

Even if she can handle it all on her own a wise woman knows how to carry herself in a manner where she always reverences her husband and esteems him highly ensuring he always feels important, needed and as though he is the captain of the ship.

If you ever want to tear down a man kill his ego, and if you ever want to build up a man stroke his ego. In some instances men are similar to women, when we get dressed we want you to tell us how fine we look and how you like how we walk in our new stilettos.

Men are the exact same way. They want to know they look nice with their new hair cut or fresh pair of Jay's or Stacy Adams. Men also enjoy praise on their accomplishments, we must remember men have feelings to and although they are to be the stronger vessel believe it or not they want to feel loved, needed and accepted.

As single women if we are going to transition into being a wife we are going to have to shift our mentality, prepare for the husband we desire, and position ourselves to be found. My pastor preached a message once in which he said, wouldn't it be a tragedy for one to transition before they transformed? Pause and think about that for a moment.

He said it is vital that we transform before we transition so that we can handle all that comes our way in the next level. The same thing applies to positioning and preparation before your mate can find you, you must first be in position and you need to be prepared.

It is during your time of singleness that you are to work on you. If you want to lose twenty pounds, if you want to save money, if you want to work on your credit, if you want to go back to school or even if you want to travel the country, do all of that while you are single for when your husband comes your focus will have to shift on caring for him and you won't always be able to do what you desire to do when you desire to do it. There's nothing worst than married women still operating as if they are single and single women operating and catering to a man as if they are married. That one is pretty self-explanatory so I'll leave that alone.

You can't be hanging out with the girls all night partying but then say you want a Kingdom man. A Kingdom man will smell that aroma of filth on you from a mile away and look right past you and reach for the sister you have deemed as unattractive and you wonder why he skipped past your big hips and thighs.

Mistake # 8: A Kingdom man is not looking for a woman whose legs are up in the night at night from having hot passionate sex. But a Kingdom man is seeking a Kingdom woman whose arms are uplifted in worship.

So often we as women believe that we have a magical power between our legs that will cause a man to never desire another woman other than us. Now, this can be true or false but that would be contingent upon your man.

If your man has lust issues and is a womanizer then what you have to offer him will satisfy him temporarily but soon and very soon he will nee another fix. One thing about lust is it is never satisfied, and it will accept what it wants from whoever, whenever.

Point # 10: Stop giving up your goodies thinking that will keep a man.

A real man of God will wait and not put you in a position to compromise Trust me sex will be much better when you wait to have it with your kin

A Kingdom woman is wise in her dealings for she understands that she i on a mission and must keep strong women around her who will support her and are assigned to her life to ensure she doesn't miss her date with her destiny. This is why it's important to have a Naomi in your life.

Mistake #9: As single woman we tend to get off track, focusing on what everyone else is doing and judging their relationship from the outside looking in. You should never envy another person's relationship for what it looks like on the outside is not always the case on the inside.

A Single Woman's Focus should be on the things of the Lord. Paul wrote that we are to be more concerned with the things of the Lord over anything else. He begins to go on to say that a married woman has to cater more to the needs of her husband but the single woman was to submit herself to things of the Lord.

> ***Point # 11:*** *Never judge a relationship by external things for you never know what she has to deal with in order to have the luxurious lifestyle you often dream of.*

As single women we should be the best servants in our churches, on our jobs and in our neighborhoods. The prayer and intercessory ministries at our churches should consist of many single women for we have more time on our hands than married women.

Now I do understand that as single women many of us may also be single mothers, which is not how Christ intended for it to be. Some of us became pregnant out of wedlock, some have children from previous marriages or perhaps you became pregnant due to the crime of rape, but whatever your story know that there are no excuses, for you too can serve in the Lord with gladness.

Mistake # 10: Another mistake I see single women make is when dating they try to rush the dating process. When you meet a nice guy, take your time getting to know him. As you date, be on guard, pay attention and collect data.

Now I'm not saying be so uptight where you are not enjoyable, but at the same time don't be so loose and comfortable where you are talking more than you are listening. The purpose of dating is to take your time and get to know someone to see if you really like them past all of the surface things.

Many times ladies we can like a man when we first see him because we are charmed by his nice smile like Justin Timberlake, or his dark chocolate skin like Morris Chestnut. Or perhaps you are turned on by a man with a muscular build such as Usher or The Rock.

Whatsoever your preference you must not be blind by the outer appearance and pay attention to more essential things such as his manners his choice of words, is he too forward, how does he treat the waitress. Is he flirty? Listen with your ears rather than with your eyes.

You may be thinking, listen with my ears rather than my eyes? Yes you heard me correctly. Often time men can be saying, *"I don't want a relationship"* or *"I'm not looking for anything serious".* Or *"I'm not really into titles. What's wrong with just kicking it?"*

We all know what the term just kicking it means; or in the words off Musiq Soulchild: *"My B-U-D-D-Y!"* So often men are up front and hone with us but because we are blinded by his outer appearance and honestly wish we could forget we were a Christian, or a Minister, Pastor, Head Deacon; etc. and get our freak on. Trust me I have been there!

But once you focus on the physical too much you then open your soul up to being led by your flesh rather than the spirit. See, David seeing Bathsheba wasn't the sin; it wasn't until he continued to gaze (or stare) at her that he committed adultery in his heart.

Point # 12: *When dating guard your ear and eye gate for they both lead your soul and you must protect your spirit at all cost.*

Once the wrong thing enters into your heart, it is hard to get rid of it! No only must you resist trying to rush through the dating process but you must also be careful and on guard against the brother who tries to pressure you into moving forward when you have known him all of five minutes.

Don't get me wrong there are still a lot of good men out here however, some of the things I am sharing with you applies to them as well. So often men truly desire to be loved and once they meet a nice woman or feel they have heard the Lord tell them, *"This is your wife,"* they tend to want to skip the necessary process or steps of dating and take time to get to know the woman.

Point # 13: *Never allow a man to add pressure to you by telling you, "God said you are my wife." Trust me, if God told him, he'll tell you as well.*

Never think that men have it all together, trust me they too have been hurt, desire to be loved and are tired of games. Don't allow their tough outer layer to fool you. Most men are just as loving as we are however, it is how we desire to display our love that makes up the difference.

Mistake #11: Don't think the Lord is going to send your husband while you are with someone else husband!

Ouch! I know that one is tough but I must give it to you raw. A lot of single women are out here laying with someone else husband calling him "Mr. Right Now" while waiting on "Mr. Right".

Can I tell you a secret? If you are with someone else's husband (meaning he is still married and has yet to be divorced) don't think the Lord is going to send the mate you desire while being laid up with another woman's husband.

I'm sure you may be wondering what qualifies me to speak on this topic. I can't encourage you from a place in which I have not yet walked. I used to be the type of woman who thought it was okay to date a man who was still married to his wife although they were living in separate homes, or sleeping in separate bedrooms.

35

Ladies settling for these type of relationships always end in disaster! If you settle for second place now don't expect first place later. We as women must think more highly of ourselves and stop believing the statistics that tell us there are ten women to each man. Now although this may be true in the natural, I still choose to believe that every woman who desires a husband God has someone just for you.

Point #14: *Don't settle for second place now but expect to be in first place later.*

If you are a woman who is currently dating a man who has a wife I want to challenge you to take a moment and think of all of the seeds you are sowing and know that what you sow you will also reap.

If that man truly desires or even loves you he will want to do it the right way which is by first finishing the process of divorcing his wife and then pursuing you. As a woman of God you must know that you are worth it and that you do no have to settle or compromise in order to be happy.

Point # 15: *Don't fall for a man who is married but says him and his wife are having problems and he is unhappy. If he really wants you he will leave and marry you.*

I also want to encourage you to be careful of the vulnerable moments you have and with whom you have them with. You must protect yourself at all times and not become so lonely or desperate that you settle for a man who is with someone else.

Too many women are either taking care of men or settling for gifts or enjoying great sex from a man who is not committed to them. We must know that we are worth more, deserve more and should require more. But in order to gain more you must require more.

As it relates to dating, it's important to build a solid friendship first which ultimately makes your relationship stronger. So ladies, don't rush the process but take time to get to know the individual first and don't be afraid to pay attention to red flags and follow the leading of the Holy Spirit, and trusting Him to guide you.

Notice I did not say anything about follow your heart? The Bible tells us that our heart is deceitful and we can't trust anything it tells us. Therefore, again do not follow your heart but the leading of the Holy Spirit and commit to being led by our spirit and not our flesh.

Not only is there no good thing within our flesh but following our flesh will lead us into deception or better yet to death. I encourage you not to get so caught up in wanting a mate so badly that you are willing to settle or compromise who you are for temporary comfort.
Many women are moving ahead of God in an effort to make things happen for themselves. I believe as singles we must get back to a place of praying and petitioning God, knowing that whatsoever we ask in His name He will grant in His timing.

We as single women must grow to a place in life where although God's Word is full of promises we must develop spiritual maturity knowing that His ways are not our ways and His thoughts are not our thoughts. In return, we must not only trust His timing but also learn how to rest in Him.

When you really begin to rest in God your spirit becomes calm, relaxed and anxiousness flees. In doing so, you will make better choices in your friendships, business, disciplining your children, operating in ministry and your overall life; etc. We must learn how to not only wait on God but to also how to wait in him.

Juanita Bynum has a song called, *Don't Mind Waiting* and many of us sing this song so beautifully however we fail to really grab hold of what the song is truly saying and trust God to give us what we need when we need it.

We must know again that everything we need God has it and will supply it in due time. There's another song that says, "He may not come when you want Him but He will be there right on time." We must know that God is not playing and is not a God who sleeps nor slumbers but He is alert and is very well aware of all that is taking place in your life. He has it all under control and will grant you the very desires of your heart when you are well prepared for them.

Know that any blessing received prematurely could end up doing more damage to you than good. This is why preparation and positioning are vitally important during your process as a single woman and that is why am writing about A Single Woman's Focus to get your attention on the Kingdom versus on the mere fact that your flesh wants a man!

Mistake # 12: Another mistake many single women make is mistaking their assignment from their husband. As a single woman you must understand that every man you will meet is not your husband.

Point #16: Don't mistake your assignment from your husband; know the difference!

In this hour it is necessary that you know who is who in your life and that you be able to clearly define each of them and their designated place in your life. I can remember one of the ministers at my church teaching on the topic of identifying people in your life and one point was separating constituents from confidantes and being sure not to confuse the two. The same is necessary as it relates to being able to identify your mate from your assignment. You may ask, "Well who is to say he won't start out as my assignment and later become my husband?"

My sister, I have no problem with this question and my reply is simple. Your assignment may very well end up being your husband but my dilemma is often time as women we don't allow time to be the determining factor. We often go in with a preconceived notion thinking that we can change a man which is truly not the case!

A scripture I have witnessed many women use in the Bible is the one which tells us the sanctified wife sanctifies the husband, however, what the key word in that sentence? You got it! The key word is wife! Stop trying to change a man who doesn't belong to you in the first place!

Better yet, we don't even possess the power to change ourselves so what makes us believe we have the power to change someone else? We must learn that God has a unique plan for our lives.

According to Jeremiah 29:11 He is not trying to figure it out but He already had your entire life mapped out before the foundation of the world. We must again learn to trust God's timing while we prepare and position ourselves for our time of transition into marriage.

Mistake #13: Stop playing the role of a wife without a ring!
As women we must stop giving a man so much during our time of dating. All he should receive during your courtship is your conversation, a portion of your time and your friendship if you desire to extend it; not what lies below your belly button.

Point # 17: *If he really wants or desires you, he'll put a ring on it!*

We must learn how to properly date which simply means we are to be storing data about the person of the opposite sex in which we are interested in. It takes time to build a friendship therefore it will take time to transition into marriage.

I know the Bible tells us that God created the world in six days and rested on the seventh. However, don't forget that one day here on earth is as a thousand days unto the Lord. Be patient, take time to learn more than just his first name, what he drives, what size shoe he wears and whether or not he is bowlegged. I'm laughing and I'm sure you are too but you know I'm telling the truth!

Often times we tend to focus more on temporal or physical things rather than focusing on what really matters such as: whether or not he is a Christian, is he faithful to his local church, how does he treat his mother and/or sisters, does he have children (if so, does he take care of them), is he a man of prayer, a man of integrity, a man of faith; etc. These are the things we should be praying and believing God for due to the fact that marriage is ministry and you want someone who will compliment you not complete you.

R & B artist, Keyshia Cole came out with the song, "You Complete Me" however God's word tells us that in Christ we are complete for without Him we can do nothing. Our mate should be an added accessory, our cherry on top, the exclamation point to our flavoring sentence!

Beyonce' also had a song called, "Me, Myself & I" encouraging women to be independent and self –reliant. Ladies, this is not the way to go. We were designed for relationships and we must learn first who we are and what our purpose is before we connect ourselves to another individual. W were created for relationships, but more importantly we were created to have a relationship with our Lord and Savior Jesus Christ above all else.

My point is it's time to know who you and whose you are and refuse to settle for anything less than God's best! Wouldn't it be something if all th women around the world raised their standards and refused to be the mistress, the side chick, cuddle buddy or any of that nonsense, and really challenged our men to arise and be the men they were created to be simply by us being the Kingdom women we were created to be?

So often we as women want to degrade our men by describing them as dead beat fathers, homosexuals, womanizers; etc. however, that is not *all* men. As a woman of prayer who seeks the Lord with great expectation you must be mindful of the words you speak, knowing that they have power and will produce either death or life. The choice is yours! I choose to speak life!

Mistake # 14: Another mistake single women make is settling for a man who is not really your man at all but somehow you have adapted the mentality, *"Any man is better than no man at all."*

Prior to writing today, I began to flip through the channels on television and to my surprise guess what movie was on? *Waiting to Exhale!* Immediately I was like, "Ok God I hear you!" In case you are not familiar with the movie: *Waiting to Exhale,* it began as a book written by Terry McMillan and later evolved into a movie directed by Forest Whitaker.

The movie is about four friends who all have relationship problems. Bernadine Harris (played by Angela Bassett) was a middle-aged African American woman who was once happily married to the man of her dreams (or so she thought) for 11 years. She had birthed two beautiful children with him only to later have him leave her for a Caucasian woman.

Savannah Jackson (played by the late Whitney Houston) was a beautiful woman at the peak of her career who found herself in a love triangle with a married man who always promised to leave his wife but never did.

Gloria Matthews (played by Loretta Devine) was a beautiful, plus sized, woman who learned the father of her son was now a homosexual and which threw her for a loop and she too struggled with finding a man she could keep (or better yet worth keeping).

Lastly, there was Robin Stokes (played by Lela Rochon); out of four friends Robin had it the worst. On the outside, she was a beautiful woman who appeared to have it going on but Robin had a thorn in her flesh identified as a tall, dark, handsome man named Russell.

Russell was married and was another man who claimed he was going to leave his wife and although Robin knew that would never happen she continued to entertain conversations and spend evenings with him. These times consisted of her opening herself up sexually and emotionally to him knowing that nothing would ever transpire from their relationship.

How many women do you think are committing adultery with a man who claims he is going to leave his wife due to him being unhappy? Perhaps their reasoning of remaining there is because of their kids, what others may think if they divorced or perhaps the marriage was great but he had unresolved issues within himself which as a result caused him to cheat on his wife with multiple women.

Can I say something? If a man will cheat on his wife with you then trust and believe he will cheat on you with someone else. There are so many women who believe they are the only "chic on the side" but trust if he has you there is a possibility of there being others.

Point # 17: While waiting to exhale ensure you do not operate beneath your standards by opening yourself up to a man who has already said, "I do."

Throughout the movie it shows various men Robin dated and I recall one man not being her type at all for he was a heavy set, sloppy, an overall unattractive man. Now although he was financially well-established and Robin knew from day one she was not attracted to him, because she was lonely, she forced herself to become intimate with him for as she states in the movie, she just wanted to get her feet wet; well not exactly her feet.

What Robin truly desired was to be held, loved, and received attention from someone of the opposite sex and later settled for Troy because he was the one available at that moment without a side chic. Well, he did actually end up having one and she came in the form of drug addiction.

If you have seen the movie then I'm sure like me you too were wondering what in the world Robin was doing let alone thinking when she dated Troy. He was a drug user and Robin was a very pretty woman. I wonder how many beautiful broken women there are out there. I'm sure there are lot, I used to be one of them. I desired to be loved, touched, kissed, caressed so badly that I found myself lying with different men seeking a satisfaction that none of them could give me. My ache was internal and matter how much sex I had nothing could soothe it.

Sadly, there are a lot of women like Robin out here today who are beautiful, yet insecure, desperate for attention and longing to be loved by a man. Now there is absolutely nothing wrong with desiring to love someone as well as be loved but you must ensure you are not operating outside of the will of God by trying to make things happen on your end instead of again, trusting God's timing.

Like Robin, we must be careful the friends we have in our ear attempting to give us advice. I found it funny how Savannah who was in love with a married man, Kenneth, who always claimed he was going to leave his wife (in which he never did) had the audacity to call Robin out about dating Troy who was a drug user. Now, I don't agree with his addiction but at least he was single! This is why you need a Naomi in your life to provide godly counsel because in this situation it was definitely as if the pot was calling the kettle black!

As a woman of God we must be careful when we have friends who call themselves counseling us but yet their stuff stinks just like ours do. It is important that you ensure the friends you seek advice from don't have similar situations going on for the two of you will be like the blind leading the blind and there is only one landing place for people of this nature: the ditch!

I recommend that you spend time with elderly women who are more seasoned and have been around a lot longer than you. Often we feel they won't be able to relate because the times are different but the truth of the matter is there is nothing new under the sun and we could learn a lot from our mothers (from our churches), and elderly women who are sitting on tons of wisdom waiting for someone like you to come along and soak it up like a sponge. Again, every Ruth (you) needs a Naomi.

If you are unsure how to locate your Naomi, pray for her and the Lord will reveal who she is for this particular season of your life. Naomi's role will be detrimental to your success and you will be just fine if you will heed her words as it aligns with the Word of God.

Now, back to the movie: There is one part in which I absolutely loved! It was a scene in the movie where Bernadine was in the process of going through a divorce and was sitting at a bar having a drink trying to clear her mind and in walks Wesley Snipes' character (I fail to remember his character's name).

However, he started a conversation with Bernadine and the two of them began talking and although she was very nonchalant and didn't seem to want to be bothered at first, after a few drinks she began to open up and shared how she was in the midst of a very painful divorce.

Wesley Snipes then shared that his wife was battling cancer and after learning that the woman Bernadine's husband left her for was a Caucasian woman, he shared with her that his wife was Caucasian as well.

Here's the part that I loved. He then went on to tell her, *"I could tell you the reason why I am with her is because she is dying and I could say a whole bunch of stuff. But the truth of the matter is, I love her and she is the only woman I have ever loved."*

Girlfriend, if you have seen the movie I'm share the very tip of your spine began to tingle just as mine did! I remember hearing him say that and my mouth was wide open as I thought, *'Now that's love!'* Not only did he console Bernadine that night by spending an honest evening with her in which he refrained from touching her inappropriately neither was he sexually involved with her. He simply held her and hypothetically speaking acted as an angel to hold Bernadine and assure her that everything was going to be okay.

Now, the Christian part of me has to say, yes the gentleman was wrong for spending the night with another woman in a hotel due to the fact of him being married but the way he handled that opportunity was amazing because Bernadine was vulnerable, wounded and broken. When they arrived back to her room, she asked Wesley Snipes' character what he wanted to do and again so nicely put he responded, *"Let's make tonight beautiful."*

The movie goes on to show the two of them laying in a spoon position in the bed on top of the covers. Now, again I am not saying it was right but was glad that nothing happened and how the movie displayed Wesley Snipes' character as a great husband to his wife.

He had an opportunity to cheat but he didn't because he genuinely loved his wife although he too was hurting at that time because he was literally watching her die and he could not do anything to help her. That part of the movie was very touching to me. I believe when you have a desire to do wrong and you don't do it but you press past your flesh and obey your spirit, in return your spirit becomes stronger and your flesh is weakened. I know there are things are flesh wants however, the next time you are tempted to do something or say something you know you shouldn't do or say, tell yourself, *"No!"* and watch you become stronger.

I encourage you not to settle and end up like the four women I mentioned above who were not only all without a man but they also comforted one another and offered advice when they were in no condition to do so. This is why it's vital to have a Naomi in your life. One who will impart wisdom and speak from a place of growth, wisdom and experience rather than anger, bitterness and pain.

I also recommend that single women have diversity in their relationships. Establish relationships with women outside of your current race and another thing, if you desire to be married it would be wise to develop friendships with other faithful married women whom you can learn from.

Honestly, I believe the best way to remain single is to surround yourself with only single friends. I know you're probably like "huh?" but think about it. Have you ever wondered why millionaires hang around other millionaires?

I believe it has a lot to do with mindset. I personally have a mixture of friends where majority of them are older; some are married, some have never been married, some have experienced divorce, some have children and some don't. They key is these are different types of women who bring different experiences and wisdom in which I do not have because I have not walked in their shoes.

I remember having a conversation with a group of older women who told me, *"Baby when you get older and mature, no longer will it matter whether or not your husband looks like Shemar Moore or Morris Chestnut."* I was shocked they even knew who these men were! They went on to say, *"Once you have more experience in life, having a man who genuinely loves the Lord and loves you, will be all that matters to you."* At that time I was about 19 or 20 and thought those ladies were absolutely nuts! I remember asking them very sincerely, *"Can't he be fine and saved?"* They laughed and said *"Now baby you normally don't get both."* Back then I thought their comments were outrageous but nine years went by and I notice I was still single, I began to remember this particular conversation with these group of elderly women who laughed at me and went on to say, *"Ya'll young girls don't know nothing. You wouldn't know a good man if it slapped you in the face. All ya'll want is sex! You don't know nothing about a real marriage!"*

Although what those ladies were saying got on my nerves sadly, it took me nine years to see exactly what they were saying. I missed several great opportunities with some awesome brothers whom I'm sure would have made excellent husbands but because my list was ridiculous and I was far from meeting any of the criteria myself that I had set out for them I remained single.

Mistake # 19: Be careful not to always judge a man by how he looks on the outside and miss out on a great man with excellent quality, character and the ability to establish a well rounded family and be the man God created just for you.

I remember years back I had silly stuff on my list such as:
- He had to be light skin (Could not be dark skinned)
- 6ft tall & up
-Nice smile
- Drive a nice car
- Have money; etc.

Notice I didn't have anything about God, his character, how he felt about family; etc and that was because I was young and immature. Guess what else? I had come across plenty of guys who fit the above "list" and guess where I ended up at? On my back and without a ring!

Point # 18: *Be careful not to miss Boaz just because he doesn't come in the package you expected him to come in.*

Always be open minded when dating, no one person will everything you desire. You will have to compromise to a certain degree. I would rather have a man who is attractive in his own way, perhaps may be shorter than I desire, but be a solid Christian man of faith, family oriented, a tither, respect and love his mother, have the spirit of a father and much more than for him to have all of the physical attributes but on the inside he is empty and is good for nothing but a great photograph and can sex me real good.

Truth of the matter is after a while the sex can get old, and although it may be good if you are having to pay all the bills, clean the house, wash his dirty clothes, take care of his kids because he doesn't have a job or yet you are getting knocked in the head every other day because of his alcohol addiction in which you haven't told anyone.

Point # 19: *Never allow the opinions of others to cause you to date someone whom they feel you should be with.*

Choose a man who makes you happy, who compliments (not completes) you and who loves your Jesus just as much if not more than you do and displays it through his actions.

Often times ladies we will overlook the brother who may treat us very well but may not have the hottest body or he may not drive the finest car and we will settle for the one that is fine as ever but slaps you around like your name is Anna Mae Bullock and he's Ike Turner!

Now that I've experienced life a little bit more the things I desire within a mate have changed tremendously.

Now, my "list" looks more like this:

Must be a TRUE Man of God

Attractive to ME (No longer matters what others think)

Faithful

Loyal

Charismatic

Manages Money Well

Loves Children

Adventurous

Remember to take the emphasis off of the man and begin to work on becoming the list you create for your mate. Doing so will ensure you are the "good thing" he has been waiting and preparing for as well.

Mistake #20: The last mistake I want to mention that single women mak is not taking the time to heal from previous relationships. I see so many women develop this "I need a man mentality" and it truly saddens my heart.

There are some women who are in their thirties and forties who have never been without a man by their side. Often times when you come across women who are like this, they have no clue who they really are, f they tend to adjust to accommodate or satisfy whatever man they are wit at the time.

This is why the season of preparation and positioning is so important because it enables you time to get to know the real you. When it comes to marriage you should not settle because you are locked into what statistics say or you don't have the proper self-image to know that you deserve better and do not have to accept every invitation that comes your way. As women we tend to hop from one relationship to another and another without taking time to heal and detox our spirits from our previous mate. When you have been hurt, abused or misused, only time and actually dealing with the issue can heal those wounds. It is truly impossible to conquer what you are not willing to confront.

But what do we do? So often (and men are guilty of it as well) we end one relationship only to end up in another one that is a lot worse than the previous one. I encourage you to take your time. So what your biological clock is ticking! Baby the God you serve can redeem the time and you will not skip a beat!

But you must get rid of anxiousness and study the Top 20 mistakes I mentioned that single women make. If you find yourself operating in any of them take a moment and identify which mistakes you are guilty of and go deeper by identifying the why?

If you are one who is currently involved with a married man, ask yourself why you do what you do? Why do you entertain this relationship? How do you really feel about yourself? What void are you trying to fill?

Perhaps you were one who gives too much to the opinions of others when dating. Listen don't allow others to choose your mate, for our mates are chosen in the spiritual realm anyway and God doesn't need any help. Sure, he provides us with free will nevertheless we should seek God every step of the way as it relates to dating to ensure we never go ahead of him and miss what he has for us.

Bonus Mistake # 21: Don't pursue the man but allow him to pursue you. Men like a chase and remember the Bible tells us a man who finds a wife finds a good thing. Focus on being that good thing and become productive (notice I did not say the word "busy") by operating in your purpose.

Remind yourself daily that you are not incomplete but you are complete in Christ and the man God has for you will find you, you focus on being prepared and ready when he arrives.

Chapter Two
Becoming "The List"

Have you ever found yourself asking or even wondering, *"Lord, when will my time come?"* as it relates to marriage? If you are anything like me I too have asked God this question numerous times. I am soon to be approaching thirty and like many women my age by the time we hit that age we expect to have been married with a few kids by then.

One thing I am learning throughout my journey as a single woman is there is a thing such as "God's Divine Timing" in which no matter how hard we pray it will not happen until God's appointed time. It's not that God doesn't hear us it's simply one or two things: (1) The person he has for you is not in a position where he can be all you have prayed for and desired; meaning he is still in his "process" or (2) You are still being prepared and positioned to be the "good thing" every man desires to have next to him.

I believe that in our mean time we are to be preparing for the man of our dreams by becoming the list we as women so often create. By now I'm sure you have created a list of all of the qualities you would like for your husband to possess am I right? Sure I am! If you are anything like me my list once consisted of things such as: *"Lord, I want him to be this tall, make this amount of money, drive this type of car" and so forth."*

It wasn't until I grew older, began to mature and experience life that I learned those things really didn't matter because they were all temporal (meaning temporary and could change at any given time). I am a firm believer that it is possible to meet a man who is in his process to becoming great and if you cancel him out you could very well miss the man of you've desired all of your life.

Sure he may not look like much upon meeting him but if he has potential, direction, spiritual and physical qualities then I'm sure you can work with him! We as women must stop expecting the total package to just show up without a spot or wrinkle as if we ourselves have it all together.

If we would be honest with ourselves often times as women we set the bar for men entirely too high when we ourselves fall short of several things on the list. Ouch! I know that hurt but it is time to be real in order to excel in life as it relates to dating, love and marriage. We must stop expecting what we ourselves can't deliver. Now, that was good! I almost gave myself a high five!

I admit at one time my focus was on the wrong things when it came to choosing the right man. I used the word choose because I believe the Lord presents us with options versus telling us who we are to marry due to our free will.

Again, once I began to mature in the things of God through my experiences here on earth that is when my desires and level of expectations began to change as it relates to qualities I desire my husband to possess. What it boils down to is what really matters.

To help you out here are a few things on my list:

- **I must be attracted to him:** Before we even get to is he saved, for me I must be attracted to him to even desire to find out whether or not he is a Christian. I'm laughing but this is so true and often times as Christian women we try to over spiritualize everything but honey the bedroom ministry is real in marriage! No matter how spiritual he is or how much he loves God if he does not turn you on (yes I said it) then you will not be satisfied with him!

Too many ladies date men whom they really aren't attracted to but remain with him due to his ability to help them maintain a lifestyle they like to have when marriage is about a covenant being made to God as well as your spouse. We are physical beings first therefore you must decide if you can stand to look at this man in the face every morning stinking breath and all. If he looks like a gorilla on a good day then baby girl you must decide if you can really handle him early in the a.m. rolling over smiling hard saying, *"Give me some shugga!"*

- He must be a true Man of God: The man God has for me must be completely souled out to Christ just like I am. He must be just as passionate for the things of God because if not my passion could be a turn off for him because I truly love God's people and I am committed to empowering them through his word, my books, coaching programs and more.

Also, being a Christian is more than just going to church. I know enough pew warmers who look good in a three piece suit and can out shout the best of them, or even hoop with the best of them (if you are accustomed to the black church then you know exactly what I mean) but is empty.

The man God has for me must be solid in his faith and prayer life for the demons I have coming after me I can't have just a regular brother. Now, other women may be able to settle for a mediocre Christian but because of the call that is upon my life I prefer a man who is more seasoned in his walk with the Lord. One who can catch me in the spirit, who can pray for me, lead the family, be a man of integrity, character, strength, loyalty and more.

- He must be family oriented: I've always desired to have my own family and the fact that I have a pre-teen daughter having a man who loves children and honors family is huge to me. I didn't grow up with my father consistent in my life or within a functional home therefore I desire a man who loves family and can shower his wife and children with love. This one is very important for me.

- He must be FUN: I do not desire to have a man who only wants to attend church service after church service or discuss the Bible all the time. That is a huge misconception for preachers or those who are leaders in their local community.

Although I am a Christian woman I enjoy doing fun things outside of the church.

The man I desire can't be holier than thou although I do desire him to be solid in his faith. I believe the reason why many Christians are unhappy is because they lack balance and don't take time to enjoy life.

It's okay to go and enjoy dinner at a jazz spot. It's okay to attend an amusement park and ride on the rides with your boo. It's okay to go skating, skiing, bowling, visit the aquarium or whatever else it is you like to do. I will not be one of those women who do nothing outside of church. I lived that life for several years after coming to Christ because I was so afraid of falling. It wasn't until I was reminded that Christ died for us to have life and to have it more abundantly that I flipped the switch from boring to adventurous.

After re-creating my list I had to shift the focus from the man I desire to myself. I had to ensure I kept myself up by caring for my skin and natural hair along with my nails, feet and overall appearance.

May I slide this in? Our men are really getting sick of all the fake hair, fake eye lashes, fake contacts and fake nails...some of us are truly losing our authenticity because we are not satisfied how we look naturally.

I know this is a sensitive topic for women because many of us don't like t deal with who we really are underneath the makeup, weave, eye lashes; etc. Now, don't get me wrong I am not against wearing these things I only want to encourage you not to lose who you really are in the midst of it all

Not long ago I went on a journey in which I titled it: Being Me Authentically. I had been wearing contacts since I was about 18 years old so much to the point that I felt ugly without them. The first day of my journey began when I was having pain in my right eye, so much so that I had to take my contacts out and I hated glasses because I wore them as a kid therefore vowed to never wear them again.

So, I go to the optometrist and the doctor tells me I have an ulcer in my right eye and that I can't wear my contacts for about three to four weeks. Upon hearing this news it sounded like she said I couldn't wear contacts again for three to four years because I was devastated! I literally sat in the chair of the doctor's office and cried. It was in that moment I learned there was a certain level of self-love I had lost because I did not feel beautiful without my natural eyes; the eyes the Lord gave me.

Now to fast forward a bit, that process taught me that I was beautiful and that God made no mistakes. I believe that if he wanted my eyes light brown or hazel he would have made them that color. I went through a process of looking myself in the mirror every day crying because I felt I looked ugly. I noticed that even when I talked to people I avoided eye contact because I hated my natural eye color so much.

It wasn't until I began to receive compliments from others on how beautiful my eyes were and how they liked them better than the contacts. The tears eventually stopped and I remember looking myself in the mirror asking the Lord to help me see what he saw in me.

As the weeks went by I began to embrace my natural eye color and began to wear clear contacts. Next, it was taking out the weave. I had been wearing fake hair for over a year not realizing that I had not worn my natural hair out in a long time therefore I decided to embrace my natural beauty all the way around and I transformed my entire look and refrained from getting relaxers and I would wear my natural curls, or press out my hair.

This process for me was all about embracing who God created me to be and learning to love myself un-apologetically. The point of me sharing all of this is to encourage you as you practice becoming the list you create, remember to love yourself unconditionally and so to the point that it doesn't matter whether you have make up on or not, your hair is done to your liking or not, whether your nails or done or not, know that you are beautiful.

Often times as women we look for men to tell us what we should be telling ourselves. Now, again I am not against wearing weave for I will still wear it every now and then myself however, I do not neglect taking care of my hair underneath.

The same with makeup many women have skin pigmentation or acne; etc. and instead of treating it we through makeup on top of it. If this is you, my encouragement is to treat your natural skin and natural hair while you add the additions to further compliment your beauty.

You must know that you are already beautiful and when you focus on becoming the list you create you will allow your internal beauty to flow from the inside out and you will indeed be irresistible.

Back to Becoming the List

After spending time with God and studying what His word says in relation to marriage it was then and only then that my perception of marriage began to change. I learned in my time with God that marriage was about much more than what shoe size my husband wore or how well he could please me sexually but that marriage is ministry!

This is one thing many are missing nowadays. People are getting married for all of the wrong reasons instead of because they truly love one another We have more people making emotional decisions and getting married to avoid loneliness only to get married to a man whose job has him away constantly or perhaps he was cheating when the two of you were only dating and something told you things would change once you married him. Right? WRONG!!

You would be surprised how many women right now have men in their beds who are not their husbands and something in their mind is leading them to believe that some man is better than no man. Baby let me tell you something; that is a lie from the pits of hell! I'd rather suffer in my flesh than to be married to the wrong man! Now can I get an amen?

When it comes to dating we must remember to date with a purpose. My pastor calls the dating process a time of collecting data. So sure he is fine but how are his manners? How does he manage his money? How does he treat his momma? Does he respect you? Does he open doors for you?

These are very important questions to consider because nine times out of ten how a man treats you prior to marriage will remain after the wedding! So often we as women try to change a man's behavior by thinking silly things such as, *"If I put it on him he won't want another woman!"*

This is indeed an immature and inaccurate statement because you do not contain the power to change or even deliver yourself therefore there is no way you can change someone else. Secondly, if a man wrestles with lust then no amount of sex you give him will keep him home with you at night.

If you thought I was going to be cute and tip toe around topics then you have picked up the wrong book! It is time for us as single women to uplift our standards and remember that honestly we are the ones in control!

We are so quick to call men dogs and no good but we contribute to their actions. We can know a man is no good and I am not talking about just intuition but your girlfriends can even tell you, *"Girl he is a dog! He has babies all around town!"* Or "Honey the last girl he was messing with he ran her credit up and drove her car until the tires almost fell off!" Even after hearing all of that, if he is fine and carries himself even halfway decent then he still has a chance of peaking a woman's curiosity. This is indeed sad but true.

I believe it goes back to when we were children and our mothers or grandmothers would tell us, *"Baby don't touch the stove because it's hot and will burn you."* Instead of listening to Momma or Nana what did we do? You got it! We touched the stove only to find out that it was even hotter than she said it would be!

Do we really have to experience things in order to learn from them? I hear people say experience is the best teacher and I disagree with that statement. because if you have women or even men in your life who are full of wisdom and are sharing with you things they have gone through, I believe we should listen to them instead of having to go out and experience the very same things when they were sharing in an effort to prevent us from having to go through those same things.

But guess what? Many of us are hardheaded and choose to do our own thing even when doing our own thing has gotten many of us into situations in which only God could get us out of.

So lady I ask you on today are you sick and tired of being sick and tired? Are you tired of experiencing failed relationships after failed relationships? If you answered yes then it is now time to do something different! You may ask "something different?" That's right, something different, beginning with getting rid of "The List" and focus on becoming it!

Now I'm sure you as well as many other women have created a list as I mentioned previously when it comes to what you desire in a mate. Now don't get me wrong, there is absolutely nothing wrong with developing a list of what you desire in a mate, however, let's take a look at your list. Where ever you have it notated what you desire in a mate I want you to pull that list out now.

After taking a look at it, I want you to answer the following questions:

-Does my list consist of temporal things such as: financial status, cars and houses? If so, I want you to "X" all of that out.

Next, if your list contains things such as "he can't have children" but you have two or three yourself; I want you to "X" that out as well.

Does your list contain things such as: "He must be this tall and in shape," but yet you are not in shape yourself? If so, I want you to "X" that out as well. By now hopefully you can see my point.

Often times as women we desire things in men that we do not possess ourselves. We desire them to make a certain amount of money when we ourselves are not good stewards over what we currently have. Believe it or not there are some women who desire a man that has never been married but yet they are on their second or third marriage.

The purpose of this exercise is to get you to focus more so on becoming what it is you desire because I believe strongly that we attract to us what we are. Because of my level of brokenness I attracted men who took advantage of me because they could tell I was longing for love and attention and often times that make women a primary target for a man to go after her for sex.

Of course, it made me angry and I called them dogs and no good. But guess what else? There were some in which I gave them exactly what they wanted in exchange for temporary comfort. It was almost as if I was prostituting my body. If I gave him sex, he would have to stay all night and hold me even if he was getting up the next morning to go back home to his family.

Even worst, perhaps he was going to get up the next day and never call me again. It's amazing to me how we as women sell ourselves short in various areas but we fail to take responsibility for our actions.

Before making decisions like these you must ask yourself is it worth it to have a man spend the night with you and rock your world and the two of you come together sexually but in the end you leave or better yet he leaves you feeling even more vulnerable and lonely than you were before he came?

Your goal should be to attract a godly man who loves the Lord the way you do if not more and one who too has standards and will not cause you to fall because he too doesn't want to disobey the Lord.

What Really Happens When You Have Sex
When a man and a woman come together sexually there is an exchange. Women are receptors (receivers) and men are depositors meaning they deposit their spirits into ours and we receive spiritually whatever they

have going on within them. There is much more that takes place in the natural than what the natural eye can see.

If that man battles addiction of any kind such as lust; it can be deposited into you. This is why the Lord intended for intercourse to be between husband and wife because He understood that during sex was created for two to become one and multiply. Society today teaches us that it's ok to live with your boyfriend and do everything husbands and wives do without the titles. We are going to get into that very heavily in the next chapters of this book.

Let's go back to the list. I want you to look at the table below and see in the left column where it states: What I Desire in a Mate and on the right you are to place a check mark to state whether you possess that specific quality or not.

This exercise is for your eyes only and I want you to be honest because this is only to make you better as an individual. Now you must answer truthfully for this to work.

The purpose of this exercise is to cause you to dig deeper as it relates to what you really desire in a mate. That's another thing lady, during your singleness it's vital that you take time to get to know yourself and what you really like and dislike so when men approach you, you don't have to waste their time or yours.

Now, I am not saying if you prefer a tall man and a good man approaches you that is of shorter stature that means you do not give him the time of day. Truthfully there are testimonies of many women who have great husbands who initially were not their type but because they gave him a chance and took time to get to know him he became the love of their life (next to Jesus). I am not telling you to do this, I'm just telling you not to exclude it.

I encourage you to take a mature approach to this assignment and allow yourself a minimum of 5-10 minutes to think about what it is you really desire in a husband.

Prior to completing this exercise notate on a separate sheet of paper what qualities are important to you then list your top 10 qualities in the table below.

WHAT I DESIRE IN A MATE:	DO I POSSESS THIS QUALITY?

Now that you have created this list how many check marks do you have for each as it relates to you possessing the same qualities? If we were to be honest, we all are a work in progress for no one has arrived.

However, if you are one whom everything you desire in a mate you already possess then lady you are indeed well on your way! If you are like me, a woman who understands I have flaws and plenty of things I can focus on as I prepare for my husband, then we can talk!

The enemy's job is to have you so consumed with wanting to be married that you miss out on an opportunity to develop a solid relationship with God that is forever evolving and growing as you grow into who you were created to be as well.

I believe that before we can ever identify the type of man we desire we must first identify what type of woman we are currently and the type of woman we desire to be. For the record these are two different people.

Within my coaching program entitled: *Defining the Pearl in You* in which I teach women how to increase their confidence and identify their self-worth and value. I always begin with the concept that before we can ever know who we are we must first come into knowledge of who Christ is for we were created in His image and likeness. Before you can know what you desire in a mate you must first know who you are.

Many of us as women are so quick to link ourselves up to others that we fail to take time and get to know our true selves. I am not referring to the face or mask we put on when we attend a Sunday morning service or bibl study.

But the real us; the "you" no one knows but you. Sadly many of us really can't stand ourselves, but yet we are so quick to become hooked up with someone else. I know you may not be feeling me right now and that's okay it's all a part of the process of learning your true focus as a single woman.

You may ask, *"How do I get to know myself?"* The answer is simple. The same way you get to know others; by spending time with them, paying attention to their responses and reactions to certain things; learning what they like and don't like; etc. You do the same things as it relates to getting to know you!

When I look back over the men I have dated they were all different. I can remember my sister saying to me one time, "Sis, I don't know what your type is!" I can recall us laughing but as I began to analyze my life in the area of dating when I prepared to write this book I noticed she was exact right. The men I dated ranged from dark to lighter skin complexion, from tall to short, to muscular build to being overweight (close to 300lbs).

As I began to review the different types of men I dated I notice they all offered something different however, they all received one common thin a single woman who had no iedea of her true self-worth, purpose or ever the first idea of what it really meant to date on purpose (or with a purpose rather).

While I dated these various men some offered their time, others offered money, sex, and others offered validation (which I always sought for as a child with my father being absent in the home).

That's another problem amongst women today, many of us grew up without fathers and we spend much of our lives trying to find men to fill the void that our natural fathers were to fill.

I remember watching Bishop T.D. Jakes' TV Show, Mind Body & Soul and he had a panel discussion which was set up as a barbershop in which he held with special guests: Keith Sweat, Lamman Rucker and several others to discuss what men talk about in the barbershops as it relates to women.

During one part of the show the audience were allowed to ask questions and one woman who was in her late forties and quite jazzy (kind of put you in the mind of Stella from How Stella Got Her Groove Back) and she wanted to know why younger men were attracted to older women. She shared how men her age never approached her but she seemed to capture the attention of younger men.

Lamman Rucker provided her with a very intelligent response that really made me think. His reply (paraphrasing) pretty much was that some men desire to date older women due to them possibly growing up without a mother who was very loving and nurturing to them and so forth (same applied to women).

This statement really made me think because I was always one who preferred older men. If a man was my age I would not look at him twice. After hearing Lamman's response I began to ask myself, *"Is this why I have always preferred to date men who were extremely older than me because I am seeking a father figure due to my father being in and out of my life?"*

I then went on to ask myself, *"Is this why I am turned off by "yes" men and turned on by a man who takes charge and instead of asking where I would like to eat, he chooses the restaurant and simply takes me there?"*

After watching Bishop Jakes' show that day it really had me thinking and I believe I got to know myself on an entirely different level. Sometimes we need to pause and ask ourselves why we like what we like as well as why we respond/react to certain things the way we do.

While doing some soul searching I was able to identify there was a void in my life that was never filled as a little girl by my father therefore my response was more so to older men whom I became attracted to because of their ability to take charge and lead.

Spending time alone is crucial to your process of preparing to date because when we don't deal with our issues and we patty cake everything or brush it under the rug pretending it didn't happen or doesn't exist, it causes us to live in a state of denial.

It is time to experience a shift in your life in which you no longer focus on others and what they could or should be doing. But I want you to do a personal assessment of yourself and identify what your strengths are as well as your weaknesses and notate areas in which you can improve.

I admit to spending way too much time focusing on being found by the right man instead of wrapping myself up in Jesus and allowing Him to show me to the right man in His divine timing.

One thing I always share with my clients who are single women and that is you can never rush love. You can also never go out and find love but you must wait patiently for it to find you!

We as women must stop being anxious, become committed to God's plan for our lives and engage ourselves with working in the Kingdom of God which positions us to not only be found by found by the right mate.

Just as Boaz found Ruth working our mate will find us working. However, this can only happen when we take our minds off of being found and learn to just "be."

Chapter Three:

Celibacy: The New Curse Word

We are taught that relationships are give and take correct? Society teaches us to do whatever we can to keep our mate satisfied and we won't have to worry about them cheating on us or ever leaving us. Following the world' way will lead us to a place of compromise and emptiness.

There is an author who shares often with his followers that you can not make right decisions with wrong information in which I have found this t be true in several cases. Prolific Bible teacher and author, Dr. Cindy Trimm also reminds us that it is not due to an adversary that people are perishing but it is due to the lack of knowledge which the Word of God tells us.

The purpose of this chapter is to bring you back to a place of setting standards, establishing boundaries and implementation. The days of us giving a man everything he wants out of fear he will leave us are over! N longer do you have to settle or have sex with a man out of obligation or t satisfy his fleshly desire.

Do you know that you are worth much more than to be humped up and down on? You are a precious jewel; a pearl indeed; one that is not only rare to find but also whose value is far greater than you could ever imagine.

However, although this is true, we often sell ourselves short. We underestimate our ability to attract godly men or we focus on the statistic that tell us there is a shortage of men and the reason so many men are unfaithful is because there is ten women to each man.

I understand the statistics may very well be true lady however, I don't believe God allowed you to have a desire to be married to a faithful husband to tell you *"Oops! I'm all out of men daughter!"* The devil is a *liar!*

If God has placed the desire within you then trust and believe there is a man somewhere for you. But like I was told by a pastor once; he said God had a man of God just for me, but I'd have to wait patiently for him. I am still waiting just like you.

The good thing about waiting is it doesn't have to be a sad or boring process. During our waiting we should be disciplining ourselves and setting principles and boundaries in place so when we do begin to date we don't settle for anything less than what God desires for us.

Just as we each have a set of rules or principles we live by as it relates to our everyday life there are rules for dating. So often we move out of the order of God by getting the man, having the baby, and living together, then we wonder why he will go out and marry someone else. If he marries you now, what else does he truly have to look forward to?

I'm sure you have heard the phrase, *"Why would a man buy the cow when he is getting the milk for free?"* What would a man make a man commit to marry you when he can have you cook his dinner, clean his house, raise his children, iron his clothes, and don't forget, sex him real good whenever and however he wants?

Sure there are cases where some people have dated for over ten years then all of a sudden decided to get married, however, when you are a woman of God living according to the principles of the Bible we are to do things a little differently. We are encouraged to present our bodies as a living sacrifice, holy and acceptable unto the Lord.

There's a Word we don't hear much about....*holiness.*

For so long many of us thought holiness was in the length of our skirt, or how deep we could look during Sunday morning worship services. But the truth is holiness is a lifestyle! It's more about what you do when you leave the church than what you do when you are in it!

Sure your hands are lifted in praise during the service but after you leave at about ten-thirty or eleven o'clock at night your legs are lifted as well then you are not exemplifying a holy lifestyle.

Holiness is defined as the state of being holy in which holy is defined as dedicated or consecrated to God or a religious purpose, sacred.

In addition, celibacy according to Webster's Dictionary is defined as the state of abstaining from marriage and sexual relations. With the media being full of sex exploitation it is almost impossible to not be tempted to engage in sex. The way it is portrayed on television, the radio, or magazines you read having sex with a man you are not married to is considered the new norm.

I am going to say this and you may get upset with me; if you spend the majority of your time witnessing the foolish mistakes of Olivia Pope (played by Actress Kerry Washington on the TV show Scandal) when that show promotes homosexuality, lust, fornication, adultery and much more what you are doing is filling your spirit with these things which in turn comes out in your behavior or even your desires.

As singles you have to be careful guarding your eye and ear gate for what enters your heart has the ability to affect or infect your soul. It wasn't until David saw Bathsheba bathing that he desired her and planned to murder her husband just to have her all to himself. It was when he saw her that he lusted in his heart and after that it was a wrap! He had to have her!

One way to achieve being single, and submitting to holiness, and committing to remaining celibate until marriage is to be careful regarding what you allow to enter your spirit. Some shows on television you really need to stay away from as well as certain music due to the unclean spirit that are attached to them.

My favorite show is Law & Order in which I just love myself some Olivia Benson but every so often I have to turn her off because after witnessing all of those women being raped and homes being broken I find myself double locking my doors and keeping a light on nervous that someone may come in and take advantage of me.

Although this may sound weird but after watching them solve crimes for over an hour (usually two episodes back to back) it does make me nervous being a single mother home alone with my daughter.

The point I'm making is we are affected by what we see and hear whether we like it or not therefore we must guard our spirits and protect ourselves at all cost. Remember no one knows you like you.

It is time to uphold a standard and dare to be different! No longer do you have to fit in or do what others are doing to keep their man. If you are interested in a man and he tells you he doesn't desire to wait until marriage to have sex with you, then you can not be upset with him. What you need to do is listen!

One of the key reasons we as women wind up in all types of foolishness is not because men are dogs but because we don't listen. When they tell us they are not ready for a relationship but we desire to be with them, we somehow tell ourselves, "If I love him like he desires to be loved, he will change his mind." Or we say, "If I cook his dinner and show him that sister girl can throw down then maybe he will commit to me for mama always said the way to a man's heart is through his stomach."

Does any of these things sound familiar? How many times have we told ourselves if we put it on him he won't desire so much to even look at another woman. I'm sure you like me have found this not to be true.

I remember a guy I was somewhat interested in telling me that he enjoyed spending time with me and wanted us to continue hanging out and having our children around one another but he wasn't ready for a relationship. It was as if something immediately shifted within me. I was like "huh?"

But guess what? I had enough wisdom to know that I needed to listen to what this man was saying, take heed to it and not try to convince him that I was all he needed nor try to seduce him with my love potion (if you know what I mean). I needed to simply back up, reroute, re-establish boundaries and respect his decision.

How many of us actually listen when men speak? Truth is, when we enter the presence of a man we really like our first mistake is we talk entirely too much. Have you ever noticed why a man you just met or may have gone out on a few dates with will allow you to go on and on and on about yourself, or what you do or how you have been hurt?

The reason he allows this is because the more you talk, the more vulnerable he sees you as especially if you have been hurt and still bear the wounds of previous relationships.

Why is it that when we meet someone new we want to tell them all of our business anyway? Why not keep things at a surface level and communicate via common ground and focus on things the two of you may have in common such as bowling, skating, amusement parks or perhaps reading. Don't be so quick to welcome a man into your world without him earning his right to be there.

What you have is so valuable that you must learn to guard it at all cost. There are good men who are truly seeking a wife but then there are also men out here in which marriage is the last thing on their mind. Some may even play on your weaknesses but only if you allow them to. It is time to learn from our past failures and mistakes and break the cycle!

How long are we going to continue to fall into the same traps time after time? How long are you going to continue to be tricked into having sex or sharing a man with his wife? Perhaps you are the wife and you knowingly share your husband with other women.

I told you this book is no play toy I am here to help you become free in every area of your life and remind you of the pearl which resides on the inside of you. But if you can't identify your true worth how can you expect someone else to?

If you don't value your time, anointing, and your body why would you expect a man to? Men respect women who respect themselves. If you display characteristics of a godly woman of substance, character, integrity and you challenge him to put a ring on it then maybe you will be the one he takes home to mama not the one he meets at the hotel every other night.

Sure, men will try us but it is up to us to stand our ground and say no and declare the next man who lays with you, or enters inside of you will be your husband. I remember asking a married man once (whom I was sleeping with) why men cheated on their wives.

Stunned by my question for a few moments, he sat quietly as I continued. I went on to ask if it meant they were unhappy with their wives, or what? Surprisingly his answer to me was, "Because women allow us to."

I can remember sitting there feeling so cheap, low and embarrassed. We had just finished having some wild and crazy sex and here I was lying in bed with a man who told me the only reason he was cheating on his wife was because women like me allowed him to.

I can't describe into words how that made me feel but guess what? It was the truth. He didn't try to clean it up for what he had just shared was truth. Guess what else? In that moment I had a choice whether I was going to take heed to what he said, or laugh it off and slap him on the shoulder while saying, "Boy you so crazy!"

I made a decision in that moment that was the last time I would play the other woman. I decided that day I would no longer be a woman who slept with married men with an expectation that I was the only one he was seeing on the side. Just an F.Y.I. sister, they are always seeing someone else on the side. If he will cheat on his wife with you then surely you are not the only one he has his eye on.

Now do I believe the only reason men cheat is because outside women make themselves available to them? Absolutely not! However, that was the answer I needed to hear in that moment which helped snatch me out of the sin I was in. That was it for me. From that day to this I never laid with another married man and it feels great!

Am I ashamed of my past? Absolutely not! It is because of those types of experiences which enable me to speak with you regarding these matters because I have been there and done that. You don't have to be embarrassed if you have been someone's toy, or other women because today you can choose to dismiss him, repent and allow the Lord to make you over and never turn back. You can do it; I did.

From that day forward I made a vow (a promise) to the Lord that I would not lay with another man unless it was my husband. I made a vow to become celibate and wait on my husband.

Celibacy is a word or topic many of us don't like to hear much of because society teaches us that it's okay to sleep with men we date or even those whom we share a monogamous relationship with. Truth is...it's not okay.

Celibacy is identified as the new curse word because so many people think or feel it is ok to have sex before marriage. This is what we see so much of in the world today. I heard one guy say on a talk show that the way he connected with women was sexually and until he had been intimate with them he felt as if he doesn't really know them.

Once he made love to them, then and only then could he say he knew them. Now, at first I felt that was the most immature statement I had ever heard until I began to really think about it.

According to scripture, when a relationship is consummated the two become one in the spirit, therefore you do know one another in a more intimate way once penetration has taken place.

When we as single women have sex outside of marriage we lose our power and it is as if we literally toss it away. Have you ever noticed that once you have sex with a man you all of a sudden begin to put up with things that before you would not have tolerated?

All of a sudden you have stopped noticing or perhaps you then begin to notice all of the red flags that were clearly there before but because you were so blinded by his physique and how he "licked you up and down until you said stop" that you were no longer in control because you gave your personal power away.

I am going to say something and as a Christian you may not expect to hear it from me, however, here it goes. I believe strongly in the power of the "cookie.". I wanted to say something else because I believe sometime we tip toe around topics too much out of fear of offending others but "cookie" is more appropriate so let's stick with it! In the book, Act Like a Lady, Think Like a Man book, Steve Harvey identifies it as the "cookie,", so let's take a moment and discuss "The Power of the Cookie."

Below are a few steps for how to reside within your power by refraining from giving up *"the cookie":*

- **Go on group dates**: Instead of tempting yourself by being alone with this man, maybe call up one of your girlfriends and her man and double-date. This allows you to have accountability as well so even if you are feeling him and he invites you back to his place you are more prone to deny his offer since you have your home girl with you. Having accountability partners are always good.

- **Meet in public places:** Perhaps the group thing is not for you. Meeting in a public place such as a restaurant, book store, or ice cream spot are always really good places where others are present because chances are nothing is going to take place with others around.
This also protects you in case he is crazy and he is shouting out loud demanding the waitress to bring him some "skrimps" like the guy in Daddy's Little Girls with Julia (played by actress Gabrielle

Union). Meeting in public places is always a plus because you have witnesses and most men are not going to try anything around others.

- Talk on the phone for a while before agreeing to meet him: I have tried this and I can tell you it really works. You will be surprised how much data you can collect and how much you can learn from simply talking to someone.

We often times get anxious because we are so ready to fall in love but that is not something you can force. Love just happens at its appointed time and it can't be rushed or postponed. Have you ever heard the saying, "You can't help who you love?" I have found this to be true.

Take time to chat on the phone and allow the conversations to determine whether or not you desire to go on a group date or public outing with him. Usually if you do this for a period of time it allows you to get to know the person.

- Don't invite him over to your house. We as women tend to get comfortable a little too fast and we will invite a man over to our homes feeling entirely too comfortable with them after only knowing them for five minutes.

I am reminded of the movie For Colored Girls written and directed by Tyler Perry. In the movie, one of the characters were naïve and invited a gentleman over to her place for dinner. When he arrived she was cooking for him and immediately she offered to pour him a glass of wine.

Before she could turn around to offer him the wine this fool (yes called him a fool) had completely undressed and basically stood there naked as if to say, "I know what you want. I know the real reason you invited me over here."

Completely astonished and afraid, she is taken back by his boldness and aggressiveness and begins to tell him no that's not why she invited him over. He then proceeds to give her what he felt she wanted which resulted in him raping her in her own home.

Now, we could say he was wrong for raping her but let's go back; had she never invited him over so soon perhaps he would not have had the opportunity to do so.

There was a scene in the movie which she shared with a friend how she was going to invite him over and her friend jokingly mentioned that he would interpret that as her wanting sex.

The character who was raped laughed off her friend's comment and proceeded to invite him over anyway. Sure, she was completely innocent but did not operate in wisdom by inviting a stranger into her home especially when she was alone. This one bad judgment call caused her life to be changed forever.

How often do we do these things as women? We can be some of the most trusting creatures on the earth, and you can burn us repeatedly and we will always find a way to forgive. My question is why do we continue to accept the abuse?

Why continue to be misused? Why continue to put ourselves in tempting situations which will lead to us compromising, left feeling empty and having to repent to God for sinning against Him?

Have you ever considered why men can sleep with ten different women within the same week and never be called a name but a woman can sleep with five men in her life and be called a whore?

It is because of the unspoken expectation of the woman to have standards and save herself. I am not saying you have to be a virgin for many of us are far past that however, I do believe in being a born again virgin.

It is where you make a commitment to God, repent from every sexual act, ask the Lord to free you from every soul tie, loose you from every form of bondage and set you completely free in Jesus' name.

As a matter of fact, if you would like to make this pledge today pray this prayer aloud:

Dear Lord,

Thank you for the grace and mercy you have shown me. Thank you for covering me when I did not have enough sense to cover myself. Today I repent of every act of sexual immorality I have partaken in and I ask you to cleanse me from the inside out. Break every soul tie and free me from everything that is not like you. Help me to live holy and present my body as a living sacrifice.

Lord I give my physical body to you and ask that you make me over. I vow to refrain from sexual contact with any man. I vow that the next man I make love to me will be my husband. I ask you now Lord for strength to keep this commitment. I love you and thank you for being the Great I Am in my life. I will rely on your strength and not my own.

In Jesus' name,

Amen.

Date: _____
Signature: _____

Chapter Four:
Dos & Don'ts While Dating

Like parenting, there is no manual that comes along with dating, however, we do have The Bible, which instructs us to live holy and present our bodies a living sacrifice, holy and acceptable unto the Lord. But if you are like me I still had questions and I understood that I was to save myself for my husband but I struggled with the process of getting married.

What is the proper way of dating? How long should I date? What should I be doing during the dating process? If you are like me then I'm sure these very same questions went through your mind as well.

By no means am I claiming to have all of the answers however I am here to share my experience from lessons I've learned as a single woman during my process.

In this chapter I will be sharing five do's and five don'ts of the dating process. Know that I am not judging you for the only way I can speak on certain things are through my personal experiences which include areas where I have failed and others in which I have succeeded in.

Either way, I am not pointing fingers but simply providing you with tips on how to succeed at being single and hopefully prevent you from makin the same mistakes I've made on my journey to being transformed into a single woman with the qualities and attributes of a wife.

#1: Do not ignore red flags

So often during the dating process we as women desire companionship o to be loved so badly that we ignore signs that show who the individual truly is. I understand we as women tend to have a nurturing ability however we must not confuse that with our inability to change others.

He may be a nice guy but if he gets aggressive and grabs your arm roughly in the early stages of the relationship, chances are that he is abusive.

If he comes across as being possessive or controlling by trying to isolate you from family and friends, chances are he is not the man you want to be involved with. There is a difference in being protective and controlling.

A real man will share his opinion and allow you to make the decision yourself versus trying to make it for you. Sadly a lot of women end up in relationships where their mate has completely separated them from loved ones so they can manipulate and control them. You can avoid this by not being desperate and paying attention to his actions, words, and his levels of consistency.

#2: Never embrace a new relationship without proper healing from your past

I am reminded of Juanita Bynum when she taught her message, No More Sheets. She said so many women want to be married but the truth of the matter is you are not single! This one phrase threw many for a loop including myself because of her raw and uncut method that set thousands of women free in one night!

Before you can enjoy who God has for you, there has to (1) be a healing process (2) every soul tie must be broken and (3) you must be restored. We as women must stop being so quick to move on to the next man and take a moment to identify the hurt we feel from previous relationships, begin the healing process, and stop comparing every man we meet to men of our past; whether good or bad.

Your past is just that, your past, meaning it's done, over, finished! It's time for you to be honest about where you are and if you are still wounded in some areas, that is ok. At least now you can begin the process.

Paula White made a statement that was so profound. She said, *"You can not conquer what you are unwilling to confront."* The sooner you are honest about what you have gone through the sooner you can be healed and possibly meet the man of your dreams.

#3: Do not take on the role of a wife without a ring

I understand it is every girl's dream to have a fairy tale wedding however, if you notice the average wedding ceremony lasts about 15-20 minutes then it is over, and on to the reception.

Wouldn't it be a tragedy to end up married to the wrong man and then be too embarrassed to admit it, therefore you remain in the marriage suffering, unhappy, secretly battling depression?

See, all of this can be avoided if we as single women would take the time to actually enjoy the dating process. We are so quick to do all we can to keep a man yet not realize that we are the prize and they should be doing all they can to keep us. Pause and allow that to sink in for a moment. You are the prize and it is important that you know your worth.

Have you ever wondered how women end up dating a man for 10-15 years without him ever proposing to her? A lot of women have positioned themselves to be *"wifey"* or the so-called *"wife"* without the ring. They are ironing their mate's clothes, babysitting his children, cooking his dinner, and even having sex with him on the regular only to find out that they are not the only one. (In my Steve Urkel voice), *"Oops, did I say that?"* Yes I did!

Now like never before is the time for us as women to know and understand our worth and value. The truth is we are so quick to call men dogs and say they are cheaters but they can't do no more than we allow them to do.

If more women would require a commitment of marriage before opening their legs to our mate, then trust me the men would rise up and be men. However, because there are so many desperate, anxious women men don have to step up because they are allowed to have their cake and eat it too

Don't allow this to be you and if it is you, allow today to be your opportunity to change where you say no more and make wiser decisions.

#4: Do not get too personal too soon

Too often we as women simply talk too much. I'm sorry there was no other way for me to say it! There is a reason why we have two ears and one mouth, although many of us as women use our mouths more often than our ears.

Using our ears more often would save us a lot of heartache. Truth be told as women we can tell if a man is truly interested in us or not if we would pay close attention during the initial conversations such as what time he calls (does he call you late at night or does he respect you enough to call you at a decent hour?)

Next question: What type of conversations does he have with you? Is his focus on how pretty you are or your physical attributes? Does he have wandering eyes which seem to roam to other women or even below your neck when he talks to you?

While dating you have to pay close attention to things (not be suspicious) because often times red flags are there but we chose not to see them.

Finally, does he handle you with care? Does he open doors for you? Treat you like a lady? All of these are key factors to pay attention to. On the flip side, do you allow him to treat you like a lady by giving him the opportunity to treat you like a lady? Be sure to keep this in mind as well.

During a first date or even the first few dates you should not be discussing anything personal. Before sharing your dreams, goals, or even the fact that you are ready to settle down, first learn what the two of you have in common.

Learn what he enjoys, what his favorite foods are or his favorite musical artists. In other words, allow him to do the talking. Truth is, men can sense a desperate or thirsty woman and trust me you don't want to be identified as either.

Don't get too personal too soon. He should not know where you live, work (specifics) or anything personal until he has earned the right to know this information. You don't want to share all your personal business then you learn that he is merely your assignment, or only a friend.

As women we should stop being so open initially and enjoy different levels of friendships. Ignore the goose bumps and all of the "girl he so fine" moments and keep your flesh under control because the truth of the matter is the majority of dates start out good and it is not until you have taken the time to really get to know a person that will determine whether or not you are truly interested.

#5: Don't plan a wedding after only one date

I'm sure you laughed when you read this title. I laughed when I wrote it because I too am guilty of this. I have gone out with men and because the date went so well, I immediately began to think of our child's names, his last name on the end of mine; etc.

If I could count how many times I've done that it's quite embarrassing. That is why I am able to tell you what not to do. We often as women become involved emotionally well before men do. They may begin with physical attraction but our job is to show them there is more to us than what appears on the outside.

Every man wants what his buddy or homeboy doesn't have so your job is to do what other women refuse to do and that is withhold the "cookie" (as Steve Harvey calls it). Show him why you are worth waiting for. Remember men always want what they can't have; therefore don't be so easy.

Don't allow the mentality of "*What you don't do another woman will,*" to hold you down and discourage you. As a godly woman who desires a godly man, there will be nothing another woman can offer him that he will settle for after he has identified the jewel within you.

You are the precious pearl; the ruby that is rare to find. Don't give in like many others are doing but stand your ground, strut your stuff and show him why you are worth waiting for. What I mean by "strut your stuff" is show him the fly, godly woman you are for remember godly men are turned on by women who's hands are lifted in worship not whose legs are lifted in the bedroom.

As you take your time and get to know him, showing him that you are a woman of character, and you pass the dating process, develop a solid relationship and he pops the question, then you can begin to plan the wedding!

#6: Don't bring him around your children too soon

Now ladies I understand sometimes we can't find a baby sitter and we may really like this guy so we question when is it ok to bring a man we are dating around our children. I recall reading in a book where the author stated you should do so as soon as possible and immediately the mother in me rose up and I said, "Oh no!"

Now back in the day this may have been ok, but now with the pedophile rate increasing and our young children are being raped and molested, increasingly by people they know or trusted family or relatives; not strangers.

My advice is to ensure that you and this gentleman have a solid friendship first and you actually like each other before involving children. Also be sure that you really like him and not his image.

I remember dating a guy who was a preacher and I enjoyed him while he was up ministering, or when we were out with his family. But privately, we really didn't have a lot in common or to say to one another.

In front of his family we got along great but it was to the point where I did not enjoy being around him privately but more so when his family was together. I knew then there was an issue.

I have made the mistake of bringing my daughter around men I have dated too soon and what happens is the child gets attached to the man and when it doesn't work out between the two of you, the child is left hurt and confused wondering why Paul or John (I'm so saved, notice I only used names from men in the Bible- Ha!) isn't coming by anymore.

You then have to explain that the two of you broke up and so forth. My motto is always protect your children and until you have mutually agreed to take things to the next level. Keeping family and your children out of the picture protects you and him because as of now if it doesn't work out, it only affects the two of you.

Once you get family and children involved everyone becomes affected therefore save yourself the headache and don't be afraid to let him know your child or children are off limits.

This is my personal opinion as it relates to appropriate timing when bringing your children around a man whom you are dating. I have tried both meeting someone and bringing them around my daughter quickly or even being around their child too soon and I found myself more into the child (due to my genuine love for children) than the father. In doing so, I remained with the man even after knowing he was not the one for me because I had fell in love with his child. This was unfair to him but because the child became attached to me it was hard to break things off therefore I stayed until I could take no more.

Trust me, save yourself the headache and keep your children out of the picture until the relationship has advanced and you have decided you are going to be with this man.

Now that we have the dont's out of the way let's discuss a few things you should do while dating:

#1: DO Be Safe and Have Fun

#2: DO Establish Boundaries & Stick to Them

#3: DO Take Notes

#4: DO Respect Yourself and in Return So Will He

#5: DO Let Him Know You Are Celibate

#6: DO Take Your Time and Go At Your Own Pace

#7: DO Be Open (Not Anxious) For Love

Sometimes we can be our own worst enemy. When you are new on the dating scene it is okay to just go out and enjoy a movie without mentioning commitment or marriage. The number one way to run a man away is desperation. No man wants a desperate woman. Therefore, relax, have fun and enjoy the date.

I know in many churches you don't hear much about the dating process but we so often hear, *"You need a husband"* or *"You need a wife."* However, in order to get down the aisle we must first succeed during our time of dating. That is why I shared this information with you because I know there are no manuals to proper dating therefore, many are left to treat boyfriends as husbands and quickly assume the "wifey" role.

Before you know it, five years have passed and his response to you is *"we are just kicking it!"*

Ladies if you want to move from the "just kicking it" phase to the "this is my lady" phase and eventually "this is my wife" you must know how to be a lady at all times, be patient, remember to breathe and have fun. Also, don't make the mistake of trying to make him what you desire him to be. Nine times out of ten, what you see is what you will get and that is why I encourage you not to ignore the signs.

Many women end up in abusive relationships or where the man is cheating on them and once it all comes out they act as if they had no idea; but the truth is they did know but they ignored the signs.

Ladies don't be so anxious for a man that you are willing to settle for someone you know means you no good. Never think you can change a man because you don't have the power to change yourself let alone another human being. Maya Angelou said it best when she said, *"When a person shows you who they are, believe them!"*

A wolf can only hide in sheep's clothing for so long; eventually it will get hot. If you are too busy focusing on his hot ride, sleek attire and his pretty hair you will miss the signs because your attention is on all the wrong things. In order to build a successful relationship, both parties must be willing, however, you do not need to pressure him to want to date you or even marry you.

Keeping the Cookies in the Cookie Jar:

Earlier I shared how to remain in your power by refraining from giving up the cookie but I want to go a little bit deeper here. In order to be successful in being celibate you must really have a heart and a desire to want to serve and please the Lord. He tells us that those who love Him will also obey Him.

Therefore, if we know fornication is wrong why do so many of us continue to find ourselves indulging in sexual activity? For so long I would mistaken sex for love. Just because a man has sex with you, it doesn't mean he loves you.

A real man who loves you will too want to do things God's way and secondly will respect your decision to wait. He will not only wait with you but he will be an encouraging voice for the both of you in the proce:

I am currently in a new relationship and I'm telling you I often pinch myself because at times he really does seem too good to be true. When I tell you he is everything I prayed for and much more. He is just that! He is a man of prayer, faith, dedication, obedience and also he has the spirit of a father.

It's so amazing to me because for years all I dated were older men and when I say older I'm referring to men who were ten to fifteen years older than me. Guess what? I was avoiding the younger men to avoid the drama and the older men came with much baggage and even more drama!

Now isn't that something? When I met him, immediately I was thrown off when I learned his age. I was like no sir, you are a baby! I would always call men who were even two years younger than me babies, because we are taught that men mature much later than women. So, here I am thinking I'm super mature and this man is a few years younger than me but sharing knowledge that literally blew my mind!

So number one I was drawn by the fact that he was able to hang with me on an intellectual level. Not many guys I've met who were younger than me were speaking my language which consisted of my passion for ministry, empowering others, writing books, traveling the world; etc. But his language was parallel to mine which was amazing!

Here is another thing: You remember in my first book, *The Power in Waiting* (if you don't have it, order your copy at (www.CarlaCannon.com), I shared in Chapter 5, *Don't Let Your Mind Talk You Out of It* how we often get to analyzing and over thinking things and the relationship the Lord has brought to us we will somehow find a way to sabotage it?

Now is the time to stop it and stop it now! Often times we can be our own worst enemy. If you have a man who wants to love you, is committed to following and obeying Christ and he is not in the streets, is hard working, has character and integrity, baby girl, it doesn't get any better!

Be determined to get out of your own way and stop sabotaging your own life by focusing on the negatives versus the positives.

Another key is to know what you want so you are not constantly going out on dates with this one or that one. When you have a focused mind and you are clear on the type of man you desire, focus on pursuing your purpose until the right guy comes along versus going out on dates wasting your time when you knew the time you met him and he came up to you talking about, *"Hey shawty,"* that he was not a God's man.

Comical once again but so true! You know you have heard men say, *"Hey Mama!"* My point is don't be desperate or anxious. Remember acts of anxiousness will cause you to appear desperate even if you are not.

Now, back to keeping the cookies in the cookie jar: We as women must play our roles well as Women of Standard and stop tempting men with our skin tight apparel, wearing blouses with that extra button unbuttoned, short skirts; etc.

Men are men regardless if they are saved or unsaved and they are not blind. If you know you desire a man to get to know you and love the person that you are then why would you dress extra sexy with an effort on turning heads when you walk out of your home?

Did you know that true sexiness is an attitude versus the attire you wear? As women we have it all wrong and men aren't merely attracted to half of the things we think they are. Don't believe me? Why do you think we so often see unattractive women with gorgeous men who look like Brad Pitt or Usher.

It's because just as Musiq Soulchild said, "beauty is skin deep.". We think men are drawn to our big behinds and double -D breasts, and don't get me wrong that may capture his attention but it won't keep it!

There is nothing worse than an empty woman! I have heard men say, she was so pretty to me until she opened her mouth, or I really enjoyed her until she pulled out a pack of Newport (cigarettes) and began to light it up during dinner. True men are seeking classy women, who have morals and values that they practice daily and not just have them on paper only. Let me be the first to tell you, men can indeed spot a fake.

If you are serious about being celibate while dating trust me, I may try you just out of being a man but you must stand firm on your decision and again establish boundaries and follow them.

Here's what happens when you allow someone to get your cookies out of the cookie jar:

- Your vision is blurred and you now become blinded by particular behaviors and attitudes

- You now become one in the spirit with this person, for once consummation occurs. According to God's original plan sex was desired for marriages only.

- You now have his spirit (or spirits) on the inside of you and he also has yours on the inside of him. Having sex with a man who is not your husband opens you up to spiritual battles that you perhaps did not have prior to having sex.

- You are more prone to deal with his nonsense because as women we never want to be identified as being "loose" therefore, to keep our names from being tainted and to keep others from whispering about us we will often put up with the other women.

What happens when you keep the cookies in the cookie jar:

There is only one answer I have for you on that one! Your value increases! Trust me if I knew back in the day what I know now I would have kept my cookies in the cookie jar! Often times we allow others to play and we never intended to go as far as we did but if we would keep the seal on tight and stop playing with fire we wouldn't have to worry about being burned.

Once you have lost your virginity, true you can never naturally revert back to being a virgin ever again. I have heard of people saying, "I am a born again virgin" and I can understand their viewpoint on that because once we enter into Christ old things have passed away and all things have become new.

So although we can never regain our virginity once it is lost we can make a commitment to being abstinent until God sends our husband, not just when our "boo" comes along. I want to encourage you to take your time during the dating process, really get to know him and learn how to be his friend first.

Our problem as women is we so often mistake sex with love and intimacy when the truth of the matter is you can be intimate and show your mate that you care for them in other ways than going straight to the bedroom.

One desire I have and that I desire is to have sex with my husband for the very first time on our honeymoon and I am so determined to see this vision become a reality that I am committed to keeping my cookies in the cookie jar! Will you join me?

A Single Woman's Focus is all about being prepared and positioned to be the wife God has created you to be! Marriage is ministry and the two most important decisions you will ever make in your life are (1) Choosing Jesus Christ as your Lord and personal Savior and (2) Who you will Marry.

Those are the two most important decisions you will ever make in your life that will have the greatest impact; therefore my sister, I encourage you to choose wisely!

Chapter 5
My Journey as a Single Woman

As a single woman I have made so many mistakes in which that I will share with you in this chapter. I believe it is important to be transparent with others to show them they are not alone and that you understand what they may be facing.

Let me begin by saying I grew up with my father being inconsistent in my life therefore the love I should have received from my birth (natural) father I didn't and the things I should have learned from him I didn't as well.

When you are a young girl growing up without your father present that will cause you to seek love and attention in all the wrong places. Because I wasn't accustomed to my dad telling me how pretty I was and that I was his baby girl and so forth, every man who told me how pretty I was and showed even the slightest interest in me, I was open to giving them whatever they wanted in exchange.

Before you judge me know that we all have things in our lives that we are not proud of however, I am courageous and bold enough to share my story from a place of power rather than pain because I no longer reside in this place. I am also aware that there may be a woman reading my book whom has either relaxed her standards or let them go completely.

After hearing my story it is my prayer that she will pick her standards back up, repent and begin to love herself as she moves forward in her new life.

The Pain of My Childhood

Being a young girl I often found myself searching for love in all the wrong places which was mistake number one.

True love you never have to search for but it will find you!

I would entertain certain men because of the attention and affection I was seeking and in exchange for them taking me to a dinner or movie, spending time with me or even staying all night I would give them whatever they wanted.

I want to encourage you to share your story and never be ashamed of where you come from. Your testimony is not there to bring shame to you or your family but people are dealing with real issues and I like to believe the various situations I have found myself in were due to the hundreds of women I have to reach. How can you empower others if you can't relate to them?

The only reason I am able to impact the lives of hundreds of women with books entitled, *The Power in Waiting* is because I know what it feels like to be anxious. The reason I can and also write, A Single Woman's Focus i because I too have been distracted and on the wrong path all while claiming I wanted a husband but I was out of position.

It is so important for a daughter to receive love and validation from her father for that is where her assurance and self-esteem and confidence are developed. Every daughter needs her father but the great thing about it is we have a heavenly father who loves us and only He can fill the void within us.

I used to blame a lot of my mistakes on my father for him not fighting hard enough to be in my life. I recall feeling as though it was my dad's responsibility to be here to protect me from those who violated me when they were supposed to protect me. Now I operate in forgiveness and realize that God had me covered all the while and by His grace worse things didn't happen to me that could or should have.

I often would put myself in situations where I could have been raped or introduced to drugs; etc. but I like to think God was literally watching over me and rebuked the hands of the enemy for He promised to never p more on us than we can bear.

Long story short, due to my biological father not being present in my life, I was later physically abused by my stepfather who was supposed to love me. So, here was a man who was supposed to teach me how to tie my shoes, then later how to change a tire or the oil in my car, or better yet how to drive

Man number two came along, whom I trusted to love me but I literally watched him fight with my mother often and it caused him to also take his frustrations out on my sister and me.

So during times of "spankings," I actually received beatings and he would sit on my head to beat me claiming I was too wild and he had no time to chase me. I remember one time after a beating he had sat on my head so long that I could barely breathe and when he finally got up my nose was bleeding. I can remember my mom standing there telling him, "Don't beat her when you are mad!"

I remember feeling so alone and vulnerable during these times of my life. Here I was now a young girl without a father to love and protect her, and now a mother who was too afraid of her husband to stop him from beating her kids.

I remember having various trust issues due to this and therefore, I would have no expectations of men. They didn't trust me and I didn't trust them. I did not love myself for by this time I didn't feel worth loving. for I had experienced rejection to the umpteenth power from those who were supposed to love me.

Growing up with these various issues I pretty much used men for sex. In truth, it made me feel good temporarily but afterward I would often cry myself to sleep or find myself scrubbing my body like Stony (played by Jada Pinkett-Smith) on the movie Set It Off because she had slept with her boss to get money for her brother to attend college.

I remember crying during that scene because although there was no exchange of currency I pretty much was no better than a prostitute because I was a wounded and lonely girl who only wanted to be loved but first needed to learn how to love herself.

Experiencing Voids Only God Could Fill

After years of going around cycles of being promiscuous I began to enter very unhealthy relationships in which I knew the guys I was dating were cheating. Because I really didn't love myself, I had the mentality that any man was better than no man at all. It was as if there was a nonverbal agreement that when he and I were together, then it was all about us in that moment. Now once he left my presence, I had no clue what he was doing and honestly it was understood that I was not to ask either.

This why I am dedicated to teaching women true self-love which I do so through one of my online coaching programs entitled Defining the Pearl in You which is dedicated to leading women back to Christ and providing them with tools on how to love themselves properly, develop proper self-love, and show them how to develop a relationship with Christ which is the foundation for their entire life.

It was my relationship with God that snatched me out of all of the foolishness I was in. See, I was pretty and came from a good family but no man was going to marry me. Why? Because I gave it up too easy. All man had to do at one point of my life was smile at me and I was ready to do whatever to see him smile again or to have his attention.

This is why I teach heavily on the importance of self-love because when you don't love yourself it is impossible for you to love others. It is necessary to receive God's love in order to learn how to love yourself an embrace who Christ has created you to be.

For many years I went from one man to the next trying to fill two voids: one that only my natural father could fill and two, a void that only God could fill. I am proud to say that today my father is doing all he can to show me that he wants to be a part of me and my daughter's life.

It feels great to be able to call my dad and talk to him and ask his advice on certain things, and just to include him in things I have going on in my life. It works for both of us: It makes him feel special to have me call to share things with him and ask his opinion and it makes me feel good to have my dad included on all the great things that are going on in my life today.

Fast forwarding a bit, one day I got a glimpse of who I really was in the spirit and that was the day everything began to change! It was as if I had a Helen Baylor (Gospel Singer) moment when she was sharing her testimony of how one day she was using drugs and she told the Lord, *"I'm tired, if you'll just take away all of the drugs and the alcohol, and I'll serve you."* She said it was as if the Lord rebuked the hands of the enemy long enough for her to make an intelligent decision to serve Him.

There was a moment I had where I could literally feel the love of God all over me and it was in that moment in which I realized all that I had been searching for could only be found in my heavenly father. He was there all the while with everything I desired but I continued to overlook him.

How many of us do that? How often are we seeking certain things from God and they are right in our face all the while? Because we are so busy desiring what we want, being led by our flesh versus our spirit, we end up in all kinds of mess when God is leading us by His still, small voice in that we so often ignore.

It's never easy sharing the pain of your past however, it is at times necessary and even required by God in order to help save or transform the lives of others. As I was typing this, out to you tears were literally streaming down my face because I remember feeling lost., I can remember the abuse and to be honest, I often still have nightmares of the things my ex-stepfather used to do to my sister, my mom and I.

But guess what? I also know that healing is taking place because tears are a sign of release. Therefore, I never try to hold them in but I release them because every time I talk about it I expose more of myself and it makes the enemy weaker and the strongholds he tries to form in my life are blocked because I shine light on it.

That is the key to sharing your story sister. You have to tell it because if not the enemy, your adversary will have a stronghold over you. What is hidden in the dark has power over you but once you shine light on it its power is diminished. I share with hopes of helping others become free in their mind, body and spirit for that makes up the totality of a person.

You must know that you are worth waiting for. You must know you are lovable and you deserve to be loved. I used to think I deserved to be cheated on because of my past, and felt no man would want me if he found out about my past. Guess what? I found out that was a lie!

You must learn how to silence all of the voices from your past, be open to love and trust the Lord not to lead me astray. Instead of being fearful in your relationships focus on thinking optimistically and stand firm on God's word when He says the steps of a good man (or woman) are ordered by the Lord; know that includes you! I continually ask the Lord to lead and guide me and I specifically pray this prayer:

"Lord, I thank you for every person you have placed in my life however, if there is anyone who means me no good or who should not be in my life, show me and then give me the courage to make the appropriate decisions all while operating in wisdom."

Wisdom is the number one thing Solomon prayed for in the Bible. He had the opportunity to receive all of the riches in the world, but instead He sought the Lord for wisdom. How awesome is that?

Seeking the Lord for wisdom is the best thing you could ever do as a single woman. You need wisdom when dating and if you are a mother, you need God's wisdom to show you if that man would be a great fit for your child (or children).

When you are a mother it is no longer about you, it is about you and your child, often more so the child because there are some men who want to accept the mother but have nothing to do with the children.

Sadly many women everyday place men before their children and have the mentality that "any man is better than no man at all,", which is the furthest from the truth. I would much rather be by myself than to date a man who could not accept my daughter. You are a package deal and if he can love your children as if they are his then honey he is indeed a keeper!

It is my prayer that you have received these key nuggets from my story:

#1 Love yourself first

#2 Love God with every fiber of your being

#3 Know that only God can fill certain voids in your life

#4 Don't believe the statistics but trust God's truth

#5 Be open to love

Here are a few more nuggets:

#6 Don't miss the man God has for you by expecting him to look like all of the other men you have dated

#7 God will sometimes give you what you need versus what you want

#8 Soon you'll thank God for the prayers He did not answer

#9 Marriage is ministry

#10 Never overlook the man in his process

Advice from Single Men

I took a few moments and interviewed two single men: One a professional and the other a pastor to gain insight on their perspective as it relates to what they desire in a woman. I found their responses to be quite interesting.

The reason I decided to include this portion in my book is because women often seek the advice of other single women rather speaking directly to single men themselves to see what it is men desire, what turns them on, what turns them off and so forth.

I asked each of them the same questions and here were their responses.

Meet Pastor Roosevelt Ethridge, Jr.

Roosevelt Ethridge Jr. is a guru on relationships, love and singleness. He is a single father of one son. He is sought out by many for his piercing insight on the God's Man perspective. He is a conference speaker for both men and women. He is a pastor, entrepreneur, refined panelist, author and

friend. For more information visit: WWW.ROOSEVELTETHRIDGE.COM
as well as Facebook, Twitter, Linked In, Social Cam and You Tube.

Q & A:

What do you enjoy the most about a woman?
Women are the epitome of God's creation. My enjoyment is found in a woman's ability to nurture and provide strength. Women are unique, and I find enjoyment in hearing of the woman's evolution. Most women don't end up like they begin in life. Therefore, I find it commensurate to hear the woman testify of her triumphs.

The word *authenticity*, do you believe women of our culture (African American) are lacking or embracing this word? Please explain.
I believe that women are not lacking authenticity. I believe they overlook their authenticity when they began to compare themselves to other women. Personality is something that I deem as an oversight within the feminine culture. There are not many women who deem themselves beautiful without make-up, hair extensions, artificial nails, or even a voluptuous. However, I believe these characteristics are what make a woman authentic. Sure, she can make use of enhancements however, a woman who battles with low self-esteem will find it ludicrous to be authentic and unnecessary to classify herself as beautiful. Therefore, she will spend more time trying to become the "other" woman. So no, I don't believe African American women lack authenticity, I believe many fail to embrace it.

What do you believe are the key things women misunderstand about men?
I believe there are many presumptions that mislead women. Therefore, I will only exhaust a few of those presumptions.

1. ***Women don't understand the facets that make a man strong.*** *Men are measured in society by his social economical astuteness, his physique, his financial discipline as well as his possessions. What is not understood is: those things do not make the man. What*

makes the man is him finding his inner strength to override adversity and disadvantage.

2. **Men carry pain.** *Just because a man does not openly shed tears does not mean he is not burdened with pain. It takes a unique woman to provide a wall of security for the man to trust her with his pain.*

3. **All men are NOT dogs.** *Too many men have been labeled with this term because of his need for intimacy. The reality is some men have the mentality and maturity of a "boy." The word "boy" is a direct reflection of a young man in his adolescent years still learning life choice, and himself. A man comes into himself and knows what he is in search of. A man that is in search for his wife will always be more concrete than the guy that is in search for sex.*

What characteristics do you look for when you consider dating woman with the intent to make her your wife?
The characteristics I look for are whether she is trust worthy, consistent, healed, secure, and goal oriented. Coupled with that is she God-Fearing and if she can embrace my current roles/responsibilities in life or be turned off by them. Lastly, how does she feel about a blended family because I am a single parent of a teenage son.

What advice do you have for single women who are either (a) dating with the intent to marry or (b) are waiting patiently to be found by their mate?
(a)   *Those who are dating with the intent to marry, I would advise them to be honest with themselves. Don't try to become the "Wonder Woman" in the man's life; at some point you will not feel like fighting, fixing or protecting him from everything because you are going to want it reciprocated. If you are dating with the intent to marry, get to know the man. Finally, do not overlook the warning signs; if you find yourself not being able to love him beyond your "pet peeves" or "expectations" then it is healthy for the dating relationship to revert back to a friendship.*

(b)   *It you are waiting to be found, make sure you are not the reason that you are still waiting. The man you are waiting for may be great but know he doesn't come perfect. Perfect men are unrealistic. All men carry flaws in one or more areas of their lives. Do a self-assessment to assure that you are not being extreme in your expectations. Simply because, no matter your size, skin color, background, how many kids you have or don't have, your ability or inability to cook, strengths or weaknesses, etc. there is a man in this world who will find you attractive, appealing, sexy, spiritually right and most of all his QUEEN. There is someone out there! If you are career oriented and ministry driven, then you will have to slow down or make yourself available to date. Search your heart and make an assessment of what you want....and a man will pursue opportunities that he think he has a chance a fitting in.*

Meet Vincent K. Harris:

Vincent K. Harris is an entrepreneur, speaker, author, and investor who hold a copyright for The Monopoly System Principles. He's also a writer for Career Magazine, Women of Standard Magazine (as a Finance columnist) and content creator of his weekly YouTube channel, VinceOnBusiness. Vincent's products have proven to enhance cash flow and the mindset of businesses, authors, experts, consultants and speakers

across the nation. He teaches from personal experience as a business owner and promotes a message that speaks directly to those who realize they are more than what they've become. --- *www.VinceOnBusiness.com*

Q & A:

What do you enjoy the most about a woman?
The aspect of a woman I enjoy the most is her intelligence. Let's face it. Acting like a bimbo loses its novelty to men after high school. What I want in a potential wife is a woman who can clearly articulate an idea while providing numerous solutions to challenges, business growth and the family legacy. So be the smart, savvy woman you are! To many of us men, it's a total turn-on.

The word *authenticity*, do you believe women of our culture (African American) are lacking or embracing this word? Please explain.
Authenticity has gradually left our culture. From our outer appearances to our inner self-worth, many of us in our society lack an identity that's pure and authentic. We've been convinced that long, straight hair is the only acceptable form acceptable beauty and desirability. To the contrary, many of us men are looking for someone who can embrace the appearance God has given us from birth.

What do you believe are the key things women misunderstand about men?
Generally speaking, women believe men lack emotion and feelings. However, as men, we largely embrace emotion privately, and when it comes to the woman God has predestined for us to spend the remainder of our lives with, we outwardly express those feelings without hesitation.

What characteristics do you look for when you consider dating someone with the intent to make them your wife?
The list of characteristics I look for in a woman as a potential wife starts with her willingness to have a relationship with God, The Father. Next, I look for her ability to carry herself with class and grace. As a rule of thumb, I look for a woman who's easy on the eyes and easy on the ears.

What advice do you have for single women who are either (a) dating with the intent to marry or (b) are waiting patiently to be found by their mate?

The biggest piece of advice I can give a single woman who has the desire to be married is to surround herself with women who have been married for 10+ years and embrace them as their best friends. I would also admonish them to avoid people who believe they don't need the help of others to do something great in life as it relates to a relationship.

Testimonials of Successful Married Couples

"After 16 years of marriage I found myself facing the ultimate failure as I saw it of divorce. Broken in a million pieces I surrendered all of my broken pieces to God. I couldn't see anything good coming from my mess, but God did! After committing 6 years to God and getting lost in my purpose and allowing God to do a beautiful work in my heart God saw it was time to bring my "Happily Ever After" into my life, his name is Mark

I remember praying for God to reveal the hidden places of brokenness so that I could be completely free so that one day I could be my husband's escape and not his duty; the wind in his sail and the president of his fan club and it happened! I hid myself in God and Mark found me through God's leading. I can testify that God outdid himself!

We were both complete in Him, therefore, we compliment one another beautifully. Our first encounter over the phone began with prayer and today our marriage thrives, because we pray together daily. We are in love with God and each other deeply. What I love most is that my husband loves God more than me, which gives me the security of knowing he will always love me God's way. We are indeed living our "Happily Ever After" with God at the center of it all.

Be encouraged single ladies for it will happen for you too if you will lose yourself in God and get busy operating in purpose!"-Kimberly Jones-Pothier *(pictured with husband, Pastor Mark Pothier)* www.RealTalkKim .com

"Bishop T.C. Daniels and I are living witnesses that marriage works with Christ at the center and helm of the marriage. We both were Christians going into our marriage, and we had similar core values. These traits were key for us, because at the end of the day, we know what's really important – each other. We are not exempt from challenges, as no marriage is, so we remain intentional, purposeful, and cognizant of where we want to be.

In Amos 3:3, the Bible asks a question. Can two people walk together without agreeing on the direction? (NLT) The answer for us is NO! Early on in our marriage, I was challenged with this principle of agreeing with planting a church because I was not the biggest fan of sharing my husband with others, but I was my husband's biggest fan. We were newlyweds when he became a minister and we planted the church 5 years later.

So that's all I've known in our marriage. As his biggest supporter I have been able to compromise and vice versa. He too has been my biggest

supporter when I decided to go back to school to obtain my master's degree. We both have sacrificed. I want to encourage single women to put Christ first. I know it has been said before but in my case, when I tucked myself away in Christ, then He made me a jewel to be adorned by the one who saw my worth. One of the early teachings of a child is to share and I believe there is no greater example that God has given other than Christ whereby two people to come together and agree to share their lives with each other unconditionally."- Pastor Shree Daniels *(pictured with husband, Bishop T.C. Daniels)* **www.PowerofHisPresence.org**.

"We have been married for 19 years and been together for 22 years. We have experienced the gamut of things that typically tear most marriages apart; lack of finances, lack of health and lack of physical closeness. But we understand what is required to keep a marriage strong, and we believ if you had to choose two specific things it would be to ensure you are always loving and respecting one another, unconditionally. The Bible eve speaks of this. But know that trust and communication are equally as important. No marriage can be strong unless it has been proven out by tt incubator of tumultuous times. When you have been through some tough financial, relational and medical issues and continue to cling to one another, you develop a bond that no quick fling is worth destroying. Whe

you see a loving anointed couple in ministry together, don't be fooled into thinking they haven't been through much. Actually, we epitomize that couple; we have a marriage made in heaven after going through hell. Oh, and one final note, for anyone who thinks marriage is 50/50, you're wrong it's 100% of 100%." -Pastor John Lofton *(pictured with wife, Pastor Elaine Lofton)* www.Changeatc3.org

Word to single women: *"Ladies, respect yourself enough to wait for the right person before you give up the most precious thing God has given you. That is the last thing you should do but unfortunately it is sometimes the first thing you tend to give up. You must understand that you are worth waiting for so don't succumb to the pressures of adolescent men who only want to spill their seed and bounce. You could be wasting your time with a Bozo when your Boaz is waiting for you. Remember, it's not about finding the person you can live with, it's about finding the person you can't live without"*- Pastor John Lofton

"Danielle and I have been married for eleven years and are the proud parents of four beautiful girls. As a couple, we work together, play together and run a relationship-based organization together empowering other couples in their journey throughout life. We have a great marriage but have endured many of the common challenges most couples face today: communication issues, finances, sex, in-laws, parenting and personality conflicts. In the early part of our marriage things quickly went

from very bad to worst. Once the possibility of divorce became an option, I decided to make a change.

Like most men, I ran from the idea of seeking a counselor. However, I invested in a marriage repair program and decided to do everything the instructor said. After the initial change and several weeks of consistent behavior my emotionally-closed wife began to open up again. Slowly but surely we began to restore our fragile marriage. At that point, we made a decision to invest in our relationship by becoming marriage and family counselors. We wanted to ensure that we gained every skill necessary to make our relationship work.

Our passion for marital success birthed a desire within us to help other couples as well. Our marriage-based ministry, Couples Academy, is committed to placing couples on the path to fulfillment. Our advice for every single who is considering marriage is to gain an education. Learn what it takes to make a relationship work. Increasing your knowledge-base and applying the appropriate dating, relationship and marriage skills will ensure your future success. " - Hasani & Danielle Pettiford www.Hasani.com/www.CouplesAcademy.com

"Married 13 years ago on March 24th Charles and Aisha Adams knew it would take faith to walk this journey. Growing up on the Westside of Chicago, we survived and came out triumphant. We traveled to the South

suburbs of Chicago and made it our home. Little did we know this is when the fight would begin. Even though we were from different backgrounds, our foundation was and still is Jesus Christ.

Becoming one in our marriage was not the challenge; it was not giving up when the going got tough. Through good days, okay days, terrible days and lovely days we stuck together, no matter what. We were in it to win it! Lack and sickness were the mountains that stood in our way; however we stood on Mark 11:23-24 which says "I can guarantee this truth: This is what will be done for someone who doesn't doubt but believes what he says will happen: He can say to this mountain, 'Be uprooted and thrown into the sea,' and it will be done for him.

That's why I tell you to have faith that you have already received whatever you pray for, and it will be yours." From getting laid off twice, planning a family, trying to start a ministry and a business, death in the family, sickness attacking and major financial challenges, we were determined to stand together in faith and fight. We wouldn't allow anyone or anything to build a wedge between us. As of today we are still walking by faith and are stronger than ever and we are better known as "The Unbeatable Team"! -Aisha Adams *(pictured with husband, Charles Adams*
www.authoraishaadams.com

Acknowledgments

Lord, I thank you for being the ultimate lover of my soul. Thank you for filling every void that was in my life with your precious spirit, love, joy and peace. Thank you for being patient with me during my process of being the woman you created me to be. Lastly, thank you for showing me how to be open to love.

To my Mom, Felicia C. Hagans thank you for always believing in me and never giving up on me. I draw strength from your love and support.

To my precious daughter, Patience, thank you for being Mommy's shining star when I experienced many dark days. Your sweet hugs and kind words such as, *"Mommy it's going to be okay,"* always got me through.

To my leaders, Pastor Wil and Dr. Grace Nichols, thank you both for showing me what real love looks like. Even after 26 years the fire is still burning. Dr. Grace one thing you always said that I've never forgotten was, *"Although I am a woman in authority I am also a woman under authority!"* I learn so much from the both of you!

To one of my favorite couples whom I am growing to love deeply as spiritual parents, Pastor John and Elaine Lofton. What can I say about the two of you? I can see the passion in Pastor John's eyes when he looks at you Elder Elaine. When anyone is in the presence of you too even after being together for over 20 years you seem to still be on your honeymoon I pray the Lord sees fit to bless me with even a fragment of what the two of you have. Thank you for all of your encouraging words and Pastor Lofton a special thank you to you for accepting the offer to write the foreword for this book.

Lastly, to my readers thank you so much for purchasing this book and for trusting me to journey along with you in your process of transforming in who God has created you to be. Woman of God be encouraged knowing that you are only being prepared for who God has for you. Continue to wrap yourself in Him and don't be offended when brothers walk right pa you as if you are not there. It's not that you are not attractive but sometimes the oil is recognized a mile away. Thank the Lord for hiding you for a season for someone special who won't abuse or mishandle you. Be encouraged and know that God has a great plan for your life if you will submit to the process and focus on remaining faithful to Him, you'll one day look up and you'll be in the very presence of "him"; the man you have always dreamed of and you'll look up and say, *"Lord, I thank you for every Naomi that was placed in my life for I was in the right position to be found by the love of my life."* Selah.

About the Author

Carla R. Cannon is an ordained Minister, Certified HIScoach™ (Christian Coach), Publisher of Women of Standard Magazine, and National Best Selling Author of *The Power in Waiting*. She is dedicated to empowering and equipping women on how to transform their pain into power to better position them to operate in the plan of God for their lives.

Carla is indeed a young woman with a bright and promising future who unapologetically stands in the truth of God's word sharing with all who will have an ear to hear of the miraculous power of her Lord and Savior Jesus Christ.

"My greatest joy comes from seeing others become free from what once had them bound and then share their story from a place of power rather than pain"- says Carla R. Cannon

Get connected with her at www.CarlaCannon.com or email her directly at Carla@WomenofStandard.org. She looks forward to hearing from you!

Special Offers

Are you in need of a confidence booster? Are you tired of getting in your own way? Are you truly ready to manifest all God has placed within you? If you answered yes to any of these questions, allow me to help Define the PEARL in You via my coaching program! Visit www.CarlaCannon.com to learn more & or email me directly at Carla@WomenofStandard.org.

For only $97/Program includes (4) 60 minute audio teachings & (1) 35 page workbook (Download available after purchase)

Learn how to write a Best Selling book in just 7 days! Yes! It is possible! I did it & you can too! Visit www.CarlaCannon.com to learn how!

Learn how I wrote "The Power in Waiting" in 7 days & within 24 hours it became an Amazon Best Selling Book & later was identified as a National Best Seller for Black Christian Authors. Learn how by signing up for my program! It's time to write the book NOW! You can do it, with no stress, without going bankrupt & within 7 days! I did it! You can too!

Are you tired of reading junk? Are you looking for quality content filled with valuable information as it relates to mothers, women in ministry, business & more? Subscribe to Women of Standard Magazine by visiting www.WomenofStandard.org to be empowered!

Made in the USA
Middletown, DE
29 December 2016